Jerry Lewis |

Contemporary Film Directors

Edited by James Naremore

The Contemporary Film Directors series provides concise, well-written introductions to directors from around the world and from every level of the film industry. Its chief aims are to broaden our awareness of important artists, to give serious critical attention to their work, and to illustrate the variety and vitality of contemporary cinema. Contributors to the series include an array of internationally respected critics and academics. Each volume contains an incisive critical commentary, an informative interview with the director, and a detailed filmography.

A list of books in the series appears at the end of this book.

Jerry Lewis |

Chris Fujiwara

**UNIVERSITY
OF
ILLINOIS
PRESS**
URBANA
AND
CHICAGO

Frontispiece: *The Errand Boy*

Library of Congress Cataloging-in-Publication Data
Fujiwara, Chris.
Jerry Lewis / Chris Fujiwara.
p.   cm. — (Contemporary film directors)
Includes filmography.
Includes bibliographical references and index.
ISBN 978-0-252-03497-8 (cloth : alk. paper)
ISBN 978-0-252-07679-4 (pbk. : alk. paper)
1. Lewis, Jerry, 1926—Criticism and interpretation. I. Title.
PN1998.3.L46825F85   2009
791.43'028'092—dc22   2009026686

To Ken-ken |

Contents |

Jerry Lewis |

An American Dream |

Of Jerry Lewis's beginnings as a comedian; of his fateful first encounter with Dean Martin in Atlantic City, New Jersey, in 1946; of the overnight success of their nightclub act; of their rise to stardom in films and on television; of the mounting tensions between them that led, after sixteen films together, to their breakup in 1956; of Lewis's smooth transition to solo stardom; and of his ascent to the status of "total filmmaker" (director-producer-writer-actor) the chronicle has been told in so many books (of which Lewis's own *Dean and Me,* co-written with James Kaplan, is the best) that it is pointless to recite it again. For the purposes of this book, I wish only to retain a sense of the continuity of Lewis's work in all its stages. The original impulse of his comedy, to which he has remained faithful throughout his career, was to define his comic persona in opposition to social and cultural values embodied by another—usually a partner (Martin) or authority figure. Such a structure is traditional in American comedy: star comedians have generally played characters more inept, more innocent, more resourceful, or more downtrodden than those around them. The peculiarly modern tension that the structure takes on in Lewis's work arises from two factors. The first is a profound ambivalence: the Lewis figure may be incapable of matching the standards of the other, or he may be in an implicit revolt against them, but the other is also what the Lewis figure already is or may become. Second, in Lewis's work, the encounter between the two counterparts (or two parts of the same personality) always takes place within a context defined by the mass media and their protocols and technologies.

Before teaming with Martin, Lewis toured the vaudeville circuit with a "record act" in which he played back the recorded voices of popular and operatic singers and accompanied them with his own exaggerated pantomime. These performances undoubtedly not only parodied the sentiments the songs were meant to evoke but revealed the constructed, performed, and artificial nature of the person who was supposed to be exteriorizing these sentiments (thereby subverting the ideology of individuality). In these "Satirical Impressions in Pantomimicry," Lewis presented himself as a partial or composite being—a personality that existed because of, and through a difference from, another personality (Lewis and Kaplan 14). Foregrounding this difference exposed the fictive nature of both personalities.

The partnership with Martin—"a handsome man and a monkey"— enabled Lewis to explore this dualistic structure more anarchically and more dialectically than in his previous solo performances. In their performances together, Martin personified the male ideal, in comparison with which Lewis embodied various kinds of default and deviance. The difference between them was not merely one of quantity (as if Lewis's character merely stood lower than Martin's on a scale of masculinity and competency), nor was it a clear-cut binary opposition. As Frank Krutnik writes, Lewis, with his perpetually shifting identities, "encompasses not simply an alternative 'voice' to Martin but an alternative mode of being, a splintering multiplicity that contends with the handsome man's singularity" (Krutnik, "Sex and Slapstick" 113). I wish to explore the relationship between these two modes of being and its structural role in Lewis's work.

Paramount brought Martin and Lewis to Hollywood and put them into a variety of standard comedy-team feature-film formats: service comedies, haunted-house comedies, Western spoofs, and so on. As Lewis later wrote, the structures required by the conventional feature-length film made it "damn near impossible" for the duo to sustain the spontaneity and the communication of their pleasure in each other's performances that made their live shows so popular: "Three acts—that structure is as old as the hills. But there are parts of the human spirit that three acts can leave out. . . . Even in the best of conditions, the joy and wildness got freeze-dried. Between the script, the makeup, setups, lighting, and multiple takes, the spontaneity (which was the essence of our work) tended to wither" (Lewis and Kaplan 77, 267). The Hollywood experts who guided the Martin and Lewis films—on whom Lewis would later take satirical revenge in *The Errand Boy* (1961) and *The Patsy* (1964)—demanded only that he step in front of the camera to make his funny faces and talk in his funny voices. Enthralled by the apparatus and the techniques of cinema, Lewis took advantage of his stardom to learn about all aspects of filmmaking on the sets of his films and on the Paramount lot. (Lewis traces this fascination back to his wartime stint as an usher at the Paramount Theater in New York, when he saw studio promotional films that showed "the stars on the lot, the sound stages, the art department, the camera department, the wardrobe and makeup departments, the stars' dressing rooms, the commissary, and—most fascinating to me—the editing room" [Lewis and Kaplan 76].) On his days off from Paramount, he recruited friends to work with him on his amateur sixteen-millimeter films.

From the start, Lewis took an active part in shaping his films with Martin: on their first film, George Marshall's *My Friend Irma* (1949), he reworked the story (based on a well-known radio comedy series) with the writer, Cy Howard, to make room for a new character, to be played by Lewis (Lewis and Kaplan 85). Lewis collaborated on the scripts of several films, such as Hal Walker's *That's My Boy* (1951), without credit, and made suggestions on staging and camera coverage to the directors. He received a special credit for staging "special material in song numbers" in Marshall's *Money from Home* (1953). For an explanation of Lewis's claim to have codirected several of the Martin and Lewis films—including Norman Taurog's *Living It Up* (1954)—the reader should consult my interview with him in this volume. Despite Lewis's input and his increasing artistic ambitions, he constantly found himself frustrated by the producer Hal Wallis's insistence on sticking with established formulas. "If you want to know what kept us from blossoming and finding our highest comic potential onscreen," Lewis wrote, "I can tell you the answer in two words: Hal Wallis" (Lewis and Kaplan 157).

Though the Martin and Lewis films fail to give an adequate documentation of the partnership, even the most mediocre of them contains thematic elements or bits of material that Lewis would develop in his solo films. The best Martin and Lewis films, *Artists and Models* (1955) and *Hollywood or Bust* (1956), were made by their best director, Frank Tashlin, whom Lewis acknowledged as his mentor (and who made "a strategic decision to let [Lewis] in on the technical aspects" of filmmaking [Lewis and Kaplan 232–33]): the two films clearly belong more to Tashlin's thematic and stylistic universe than to Lewis's (though it is more difficult to say the same of the later films in which Tashlin directed Lewis).

After the breakup of the team in 1956 (prior to the release of *Hollywood or Bust,* their final film together), Lewis produced, for Paramount, his first film without Martin, *The Delicate Delinquent* (directed and written by Don McGuire), filmed in 1956 and released in 1957. For the next three years, Lewis alternated between starring in potboilers produced by his nemesis, Hal Wallis, and directed by George Marshall (*The Sad Sack,* 1957) or Norman Taurog (*Don't Give Up the Ship,* 1959; and *Visit to a Small Planet,* 1959, loosely adapted from but not much elevated by its connection with Gore Vidal's hit Broadway play) and starring in his own superior productions under Tashlin's direction: *Rock-a-Bye Baby, The Geisha Boy* (both 1958), and *Cinderfella* (1960). The last of these was a pivotal film for Lewis in its presentation of the metamorphosis of the put-upon, incompetent "Fella" (a typical rendition by Lewis of the figure he had come to call "the Idiot") into a suave and masterful prince—a metamorphosis whose profound resonances with his own career Lewis would continue to explore in his subsequent work.

In 1960, before the release of *Cinderfella,* Lewis wrote, directed, produced, and starred in *The Bellboy,* the first film on which he received credit as director. *The Bellboy* represented a risk for Lewis and Paramount: the title character, Stanley (Lewis), does not speak until the end, and the film has no plot, depicting an unconnected series of the hero's misadventures at and around the Fontainebleau Hotel in Miami, where the film was largely shot. The studio's trepidation over the film's plotlessness is reflected in the prologue, in which the fictional Paramount executive Jack Emulsion [Jack Kruschen] gamely tries to explain the unusual nature of the film. Partly funding the film himself, Lewis shot it on a fast schedule and in black-and-white (at that time, still a commercial option for Jerry Lewis comedies: *The Delicate Delinquent, The Sad Sack, Don't Give Up the Ship,* and *Visit to a Small Planet* were all in black-and-white, as would be *The Errand Boy* and *It's Only Money*). This original, experimental film was a great success.

Over the next five years, Lewis directed five more films for Paramount. For *The Ladies Man* (1961), he built a vast set (occupying two Paramount soundstages) to represent the Hollywood boarding house for aspiring actresses at which the woman-fearing Herbert (Lewis) gets a job as a houseboy. Lewis's exuberant mise-en-scène of this incredible set, in color, shows his expanding directorial confidence and ambition (see fig. 1).

In *The Errand Boy,* Lewis satirizes Hollywood filmmaking, casting himself as Morty Tashman (in an homage to his cinematic mentor, Frank Tashlin), a poster-hanger who is recruited as a studio spy and, after a series of mishaps, is made a star. Like *The Ladies Man* and *The Bellboy, The Errand Boy* is structured as a loose succession of gags. *The Nutty*

Figure 1. The introduction of the dollhouse set in *The Ladies Man.*

Professor (1963), the one Lewis film that has attained something like classic status among mainstream American critics and film historians, presents a more solid narrative. In this takeoff on *Dr. Jekyll and Mr. Hyde,* the Jekyll figure, Dr. Julius Kelp, is a clumsy, shy chemistry professor with buck teeth, thick glasses, and a frog voice; the Hyde into whom he transforms himself, Buddy Love, is a slick, vain, boorish lounge lizard. *The Patsy* (1964), another show-business satire, focuses on the business of manufacturing celebrity, with Lewis as the bellboy Stanley Belt, who is "discovered" and made into a star by the staff of a recently deceased comedian. In *The Family Jewels* (1965), Lewis plays seven roles; six are the uncles of the nine-year-old heiress Donna Peyton (Donna Butterworth), who, under the terms of her late father's will, must choose her new guardian from among them: a boat captain, a circus clown, a photographer, an airline pilot, a detective, and a gangster. The seventh role is the family chauffeur, Willard, whom Donna resolutely prefers.

During the same period in which he made these masterpieces, Lewis also starred in three films produced by his production company but directed by Tashlin—the entertaining *It's Only Money* (1962), the savage *Who's Minding the Store?* (1963), and the delirious *Disorderly Orderly* (1964)—and, reluctantly, one last film for Wallis, *Boeing Boeing* (dir. John Rich, 1965), with which Lewis ended his long Paramount tenure. All these films were reviewed more or less indistinguishably by American film critics (except that since *Boeing Boeing,* the only insignificant film among them, is a straight farce rather than slapstick comedy, Lewis, cast in a supporting role behind Tony Curtis, received praise for his restraint). On the other hand, a number of French critics, including writers for the two leading film magazines, *Cahiers du cinéma* and *Positif,* heralded Lewis as an original and important filmmaker. (The two magazines had already championed Tashlin in the 1950s.) The most tireless of Lewis's French supporters, the *Positif* and *France-Observateur* critic Robert Benayoun, would publish a major book on Lewis, *Bonjour Monsieur Lewis,* in 1972, by which time three other books had already appeared in French: Jean-Louis Leutrat and Paul Simonci's *Jerry Lewis* (1964), Noël Simsolo's *Le monde de Jerry Lewis* (1969), and Gérard Recacens's *Jerry Lewis* (1970). The enthusiasm of French intellectuals (shared by the general public) for Lewis has given rise, in the United States, to countless lazy and patronizing jokes at his expense and at that of France from unthinking, conformist pundits—gibes whose ideological nature has become unmistakable and more obnoxious than ever in a period of U.S. history that has witnessed the rebranding of "Freedom Fries."

Lewis's departure from Paramount in 1965 marked a drastic change in his fortunes as a director and star. He found a temporary home at Columbia, for which he directed *Three on a Couch* (1966), from a script by Sam Taylor that was not written for him. Attempting to modify his image, Lewis cast himself as Chris Pride, a successful artist who is offered a commission that includes an extended stay in Paris. When his psychiatrist fiancée, Elizabeth (Janet Leigh), declines to accompany him out of concern for three female patients who have an aversion to men, Chris undertakes to "cure" the three women by befriending them under different disguises. The strain of working against a conventional and limiting structure is apparent throughout the early scenes (Lewis said, "It was a challenge for me and I had to work terribly hard to adjust myself to the comedian. I needed a long time, two and a half reels, before I could let him loose" [Benayoun 180]),[1] but Lewis's triumph over the script becomes total with the first sequence in which Chris appears in the guise of the rodeo king Ringo Raintree.

In his next film for Columbia, *The Big Mouth* (1967), Lewis plays an accountant named Gerald Clamson, who, while on vacation in San Diego, becomes the target of criminals through his resemblance to gangster Sid Valentine, who has apparently been killed after absconding with some diamonds. Though based on a routine premise, *The Big Mouth* reaffirms Lewis's commitment to the absurd and his independence from Hollywood norms of narrative and characterization. Lewis reined himself in to star in *Way . . . Way Out* (dir. Gordon Douglas, 1966) for Twentieth Century–Fox and in *Don't Raise the Bridge, Lower the River* (dir. Jerry Paris, 1968) and *Hook, Line, and Sinker* (dir. George Marshall, 1969) for Columbia. The last of these three is by far the best, because of Lewis's obvious (though uncredited) participation as codirector (he also produced the film). In *Hook, Line, and Sinker*, Lewis's character, after going on a spending spree beyond his means when his physician tells him he has only a short time to live, decides to fake his own death to avoid paying the credit-card bills. The grimness of the plot is symptomatic of the darkening of Lewis's tone and concerns at the end of the sixties and the beginning of the seventies.

In 1970, he made, for United Artists, the only feature film he directed in which he did not star, *One More Time,* a sequel to Richard Donner's *Salt and Pepper* (1968), with the stars (Peter Lawford and Sammy Davis Jr.) of the earlier film re-creating their roles of the London nightclub owners Chris Pepper (Lawford) and Charlie Salt (Davis). In *One More Time,* the impecunious Chris feigns his own death while assuming the identity of his wealthy, titled identical-twin brother, who has been mysteriously murdered. Next, Lewis directed *Which Way to the Front?* (1970), in which he stars as Brendan Byers, a multimillionaire who, after being drafted but excused from service as 4-F (the film is set in 1943), forms a small private army with three other rejects and sets off with them to Europe, where he impersonates the German field marshal Kesselring, a confidant of Hitler (Sidney Miller). Warner Bros., the distributor, buried the film on its U.S. release, and its commercial failure brought an end to the twenty-one-year period during which Lewis was regularly on movie screens and to the ten-year period in which he flourished as a director. His attempt at an independent production, *The Day the Clown Cried,* which he directed in Europe in 1972, with himself in the lead role of a clown in Nazi Germany who is ordered to accompany a convoy of children to the gas chambers, ran into difficulties, including the failure of the producer, Nat Wachsberger, to meet his financial commitments. Lewis completed filming by investing his own money, but postproduction was never finished, and because of legal complications the film has not been released.

If the perception that his work as a director was peripheral to, or dependent on, his acting persona contributed to Lewis's failure to sustain his directing career after his eclipse as a film star, larger historical factors also played a part. The institution of Hollywood cinema as a purveyor of mass entertainment had made Lewis a star and nurtured his career. Throughout the 1960s, Lewis remained bound to that institution, even as he created a personal filmmaking system and style that were radically different from, and often critical of, the norms of commercial cinema. By appearing in films like *Boeing Boeing* and *Way . . . Way Out*—at once bloated and threadbare—and the routine *Don't Raise the Bridge, Lower the River,* Lewis linked himself to the inescapable general perception of a declined and culturally irrelevant Hollywood. Meanwhile, at least in the United States, no context existed for the appreciation of the originality of Lewis's directorial work. As a result, at a time when Hollywood was desperately trying to reinvent itself, Lewis had become identified with an obsolete entertainment regime.

Whether he appeared in his own films or not, Lewis's directorial style was too drastic, uncompromising, and strong for even a self-reinventing Hollywood. His one feature film in which he did not star, *One More Time*, although representative of Lewis's directorial style and concerns, was not a very good advertisement for his potential as a popular filmmaker capable of negotiating the cultural shifts of the period. It's not merely that the former Rat Packers Sammy Davis Jr. and Peter Lawford represent a retrograde, Establishment mode of entertainment. Perhaps the film needed to be purified of its plot (which, though vestigial, still remains prominent) and pushed in the direction of a pure interplay between the stars, as in John Cassavetes's *Husbands*—to name a film that Lewis didn't like, though he considered its director "an exceptional film-maker" on the strength of *Shadows, Too Late Blues,* and *Faces* (Lewis, *Total Film-Maker* 164). *One More Time* is a diagram of a film, a sketch of possibilities that were to remain unfulfilled, a marker for Lewis's silence as a filmmaker during the 1970s.

Lewis did not return to films until 1980. His comeback vehicle, *Hardly Working*, which he directed in Florida for the independent producers Igo Kantor and James J. McNamara, and in which he starred as Bo Hooper, an out-of-work circus clown, was released to considerable box-office success in Europe and (the following year) in the United States. His next film, *Smorgasbord* (1983), was sabotaged by its distributor, Warner Bros., which didn't bother to release the film theatrically in the United States, letting it emerge on TV and home video under the title *Cracking Up.* Lewis plays the disaster-prone Warren Nefron, who, when his attempts at suicide fail, seeks respite in psychiatric therapy.

In addition to the Muscular Dystrophy Association telethon, which he has hosted every Labor Day since 1966, Lewis has remained in the public eye through appearances on television, live performances, and occasional film roles (most notably in Martin Scorsese's *The King of Comedy* [1983] and Emir Kusturica's *Arizona Dream* [1993]). As a film director, he has been, sadly, inactive since "Boy," his short contribution to the 1990 omnibus *How Are the Kids? / Comment vont les enfants?*

A Structural Cinema

As may be evident from this brief survey, Lewis's cinema is independent from plot to a degree unusual in commercial cinema. The gag orientation of Lewis's work accounts partly for this independence, while also linking his work to a tradition of American film comedy in which situations and routines featuring a star comedian (or team) take precedence over an overarching narrative. In the second half of the twentieth century, Lewis is the great heir to this tradition, whose modern aspects his work highlights and extends. In his films, the gag—or, more generally, the moment, scene, episode, event, or block—distracts from and disconnects the plot. What at first looks like a plot turns out to be a line that is followed only to be snapped off after it intersects another line, as in the opening sequence of *The Family Jewels*, which (using a style reminiscent of a traditional crime film) follows an armored-car heist up to the point when it is foiled by the oblivious Willard while he is playing outfield in a kids' softball game. Throughout this exploit, Willard is unaware of the plot that he is intruding on and demolishing. The sequence is emblematic of Lewis characters' disruptive function in relation to plot, as is the scene near the end of the film in which Willard disorganizes the band of parade marchers that he commandeers in an attempt to save the kidnapped Donna (see fig. 2).

Like all narratives, the Lewisian narrative, however thwarted or vestigial it may be, poses and answers a question. But in Lewis's work, the question becomes forgotten or displaced. In *The Ladies Man,* the master question—Can Herbert get over his problem with women?—is simply dismissed, as Herbert finds himself in a house surrounded by women who overcome his reluctance and persuade him to stay. From this point on—despite token references to the initial psychological configuration, as Herbert attempts periodically to leave the house—the film is free to be about something else, or a succession of something elses. *The Ladies Man* becomes an elaborate, astonishing mise-en-scène of encounters, frightening, harassing, or pleasant, with the women of the house, as Herbert tries out a variety of roles: surrogate child for the housekeeper, Katie (Kathleen Freeman); mailman for the girls in a long sequence; prey to Miss Cartilage (Sylvia Lewis), the mysterious denizen of a forbidden room into which Herbert, at length, ventures; put-upon rehearsal partner for the aspiring

Figure 2. The disorganized marchers
in *The Family Jewels.*

actresses; performer in a revue staged for a TV show; and even teacher and mentor to Fay (Pat Stanley), the depressive ugly duckling among the glamorous boarders. The playing of these multiple roles appears to be an exercise that Lewis/Herbert indulges in for its own sake—that is, simply as *play* rather than as some program of self-healing in an effort to resolve the initial problem.

The studio executives in *The Errand Boy* wish to find out why Para-mutual Studios is losing money, but it is not clear that their goal is communicated to Morty (from whom they nonetheless expect information on the subject). Late in the film, in his magical conversation with Magnolia, an ostrich puppet that speaks in the voice of a southern belle, Morty mentions vaguely that he has been unsuccessful in finding the desired information, a project to which he never appears to devote any time or effort. As in *The Ladies Man,* the apparent premise of the plot proves unreliable as an instruction for viewing the film; the premise is an order that the Lewis character does not follow. To frustrate expectations further, *The Ladies Man* and *The Errand Boy* hint at, only to break off, the development of a romantic couple (between Herbert and Fay in the former and—however unlikely—between Morty and Magnolia in the latter).

Even when they have relatively strong plots, Lewis's films subvert or refuse the traditional role of the plot in organizing events. In *The Family*

Jewels, after establishing a central question—Which uncle will Donna choose as her guardian?—that allows the film to take an episodic form, Lewis lets the final episode (involving the gangster Uncle Bugsy) expand to fill the available narrative space, though its own narrative impetus serves only as a pretext for a series of non sequiturs and independent gags (the detective Skylock's unexpected triumph over a pool hustler [Robert Strauss] in a waterfront poolroom; Bugsy and Donna whiling away time in his hideout; Willard leading the marchers). In *The Patsy* (whose central question—Can Stanley become a star?—is answered in advance by the mere fact that he is played by Lewis), the duration of such scenes as Stanley's stand-up performance at the Copa Café drains them of narrative purpose and causality, installing instead a logic of the situation, moment, or event. The idea of the goal is always criticized and diverted. In *Three on a Couch,* the stated objective—to "cure" the three patients—proves wholly inadequate as an explanation or justification for the zaniness that transpires (just as in Mario Bava's *Sei donne per l'assassino* [1964], the explicit motive for the murders of a group of models is absurdly incommensurate with their atrocity).

Throughout the vertiginous disorder of *The Big Mouth,* the periodic appearances of the onscreen narrator (Frank DeVol)—who from the waist up appears to be wearing normal business attire but turns out to be wearing no pants—ridicule his own assertion that a true story is being narrated. Not only is it incredible that the story is "true," but it can even be doubted that what happens in the film is truly a "story." Though Lewis hints that the problem of the narrative should be seen in broader terms as one of communication, his treatment of the theme undermines such a perspective. At his initial seaside encounter with his double, Valentine, Clamson repeatedly tries to run away before Valentine has finished explaining the location of the stolen diamonds. Later, Clamson's frustrations with a phone operator keep him from calling the police, and when they materialize anyway on a highway, the officers prove less interested in hearing his story than in arguing among themselves about the code number of the infraction for which he is to be written up. "My problem," he says, trying to explain it to the sympathetic Suzie (Susan Bay) as if it were a chronic condition he carries with him. In the final scene, when the two reach the place (the sea) where, as he says, "it all started," Suzie says to Clamson: "You mean the problem. The thing you've been trying to tell me. The thing that's kept us running until there's no place to run any more. And chased by half the population. Jerry, I'm listening." What has to be communicated is finally dismissed (the last line in the film: "It wasn't important"). Posed in the most general—indeed, universal—terms, Clamson's "problem" is a formality, a MacGuffin, something to justify a one-hundred-minute film. All the problems in Lewis's films are like this. He insists on highlighting the fictive, ceremonial, obligatory nature of problems and then lets them disappear from the film. It is a way of saying that the problem is a pretext, a symptom.

Lewis ignores the initial premises of *Hardly Working* and *Cracking Up* at will; by a certain point, it becomes hard to tell what each of these remarkable late works is supposed to be about. After a first half that consists mainly of Bo taking on a series of jobs, the second half of *Hardly Working,* in which he gets hired at the post office and gradually masters his function, unrolls amid mounting ambiguity and disorder. Emphasis is placed, briefly, on the misunderstanding by two of Bo's superiors at the post office, Balling (Alex Henteloff) and Frank (Harold J. Stone), that Bo has influential friends who have helped him get the job; in fact, Bo's waspish brother-in-law (Roger C. Carmel) called in a favor to get Bo out of the house. The misunderstanding leads nowhere and remains a mysteriously unresolved sidetrack in the plot, symptomatic of a general sense that the film has a secret concern that it refuses to address openly but that surfaces, for example, in Bo's strong negative reaction when his coworker Steve (Steve Franken) calls him a "clown." Has Bo rejected, falsely, his past as a clown, and is the film concerned with his eventual acceptance of his true path? Or is the word "clown" still sacred for Bo, and does he object to its utterance in the profane confines of the post office? It is clear only that Bo's decision to put on his clown makeup and suit on his last delivery run is as much a reintegration as a defiance: Bo is returning to his true calling.[2]

Cracking Up begins by setting up the situation of the "misfit" Warren Nefron entering therapy with a psychiatrist, Jonas Pletchick (Herb Edelman), in the hope of freeing himself from his vaguely defined disorder. Warren's therapy sessions (with which the film intersperses episodes that are either related by Warren to his doctor or in which he takes part outside therapy) form the main line in a plot that is loose even by Lewis's standards, since the central character of an episode might be

Warren's father, a French ancestor, another doctor whom Warren meets by chance, or a country sheriff whose car passes Warren's on the road (all figures played by Lewis). The organizing principle of the narrative proves to be Lewis's presence as actor and its propensity for triggering destruction, confusion, and chaos.

Like Warren's French ancestor, who concocts an elaborate plan to escape from prison, the characters Lewis plays in all his films are in a state of flight. This condition is so basic to their existence that it doesn't matter if the flight is carried out by another (in the Frenchman's case, a cloth dummy). The possibility for flight to be communicated and delegated to another is more fundamental in Lewis's cinema than the identity of the person who carries it out. Lewisian flight is always implicitly a flight *from* something, even when it's posed as a flight *toward* something. In *The Big Mouth*, it's both: Clamson is in flight from the crooks *and* in search of the diamonds. In *Which Way to the Front?*, Byers, fleeing from the dread word "rejection," embarks on a mission that takes him into the stronghold of the Nazi high command.

The Lewis character in his later films is destined to be followed by those who adore him (Bo delivering the mail in clown makeup and costume in *Hardly Working*—an action that resonates with the unseen *The Day the Clown Cried*) and for whom he is a leader, a model, a liberation (as he is for the clientele of the Purple Pit in *The Nutty Professor*), or chased by those who want to kill him (*The Big Mouth*) because his very existence is an intolerable violation, because he has crossed a line and committed some unspeakable treason against humanity. *Which Way to the Front?* also poses the Lewis character in relation to mass movements and militarization. Rejected as 4-F (as was Lewis in real life) and cast out of the American military mass movement, Byers develops his own movement from which he proceeds to imitate and subvert the German military mass movement.

In *The Bellboy*, a truculent customer traces a line across the floor of the hotel lobby with Stanley's body by dragging it across the floor and down the stairs. In *The Nutty Professor* and *The Big Mouth*, shots of footprints render the passages of bodies through space in diagrammatic fashion. Sometimes the human trajectory in Lewis violates the laws of gravity and human limitations; sometimes it breaks off and turns back on itself, like the narrative trajectories of *The Errand Boy* and *The Patsy*—circular films that take us, at the end, to the place and the action of their beginnings. The same is true of *The Big Mouth,* with the return to the ocean.

A typical trajectory in Lewis's cinema is a running to and fro, a starting-off in one direction only to turn back confusedly, what Maurice Blanchot calls "a dis-cursus—a broken, interrupted course that . . . imposes the idea of the fragment as a form of coherence" (*Infinite Conversation* 4). "Discursus," in Latin, comes from "discurrere," which literally means to run to and fro (the "dis-" is "separative," according to Eric Partridge [125])—and this is what Lewis does in his films (as in the shot in *The Ladies Man* of several Herberts fleeing up multiple sets of stairs). In *The Big Mouth,* the hotel manager (Del Moore) describes his mysterious persecutor as a "road runner." At the end of *Cracking Up,* the psychiatrist shows that he has inherited his patient's strange disorder by running around ineffectually in various directions in the middle of a street where he has inadvertently caused a car accident. His broken and scattered movements recall those of the parade marchers under the direction of Willard in *The Family Jewels.* The prevalence of such movements in Lewis's cinema indicates that if modernity is defined as a condition of interruption, Lewis's is an exemplary modern cinema.

In his interview with me, Lewis said, of a scene in *The Family Jewels,* "I'm coming from something to that, and from that going to something. So I always did everything as an arc. I never did this without hanging here and groping there. Any good director that has any quality or any competency at all does not work on the one setup. He's coming from where he was and groping to where he's going, in order for that to work right." This kind of emotional pulse, which is indeed powerful in Lewis's films, has little in common with the seamless flow associated with Hollywood narrative cinema. He constructs his films as sets of boxes or building blocks—"the fragment as a form of coherence," in Blanchot's phrase—inside which the "hanging here and groping there" take place. As Lewis recognizes, his directorial style promotes a certain "incongruity" that leads to laughter: "I think and deal in visual terms, as Chaplin did, though I am not placing myself in his company. The benefits of thinking comedy in visual terms, as opposed to verbal terms, opens [*sic*] the door to incongruity and then to laughter" (Lewis, *Total Film-Maker* 182).

The block structure of Lewis's narratives is mirrored in his sets, which are assemblies of adjoining compartments. The most elaborate of these spaces is the enormous dollhouse set, with its absent fourth wall, in *The Ladies Man*. This famous construction pushes to an extreme a principle of Lewis's work with cinematic space: to make the borders between areas visible, letting the audience perceive the constructed nature of the space. A shot of the multitude of women coming downstairs for breakfast in the magisterial morning sequence in *The Ladies Man* first discloses the dollhouse nature of the set, with a composition that shows the cafeteria as a large enclosed space at screen right, the hall in depth, and the stairs in a narrow enclosed space at left. A few moments later, Herbert's descent down the stairs occasions a still more extreme statement of the scale and complexity of the set, as the camera cranes back to show almost the whole of the house. Throughout the film, Lewis uses the set simultaneously to make visible and to glide over with his camera the divisions between rooms and corridors. He does the same thing at the end of the prom sequence in *The Nutty Professor*, when, after Kelp addresses the audience and shambles offstage, a lateral tracking shot finds him alone backstage.

Like any competent director, Lewis is also capable of linking one block to another (in *The Errand Boy*, Morty, turning a corner to knock over a group of men in armor, is still carrying his basketball from the preceding episode) or of filling in the spaces between blocks to present a surface of naturalism. *The Nutty Professor* is the most seamless of Lewis's films, followed (also chronologically) by *The Patsy, The Family Jewels*, and *Three on a Couch*. Nevertheless, all these films have unusually consequential gaps, and the more one knows Lewis's work, the more important the gaps become, and the less meaningful seem his few concessions to the conventional requirement that they be filled.

In films such as *The Bellboy, The Errand Boy*, and *Cracking Up*, such concessions disappear altogether. Serge Daney writes of *Which Way to the Front?* that "not only does Lewis seem no longer to worry about the articulations of his narrative, . . . but it's the very principle of all diegesis that he seems to leave up to chance, the question: how (by what right) to pass from one thing to another?" (61). In discarding the surface logic of narrative and verisimilitude, Lewis's cinema foregrounds its own structural logic. The viewer of a Lewis film follows the unfolding and application of the rules of construction that belong to the film—rules that are independent of the demands of narrative. This is Lewis's formalist, materialist side. A sequence in *The Bellboy* merely stages, in succession, all four possible permutations of dual roles played by Milton Berle and Jerry Lewis: Lewis-as-Stanley/Berle-as-himself, Berle-as-himself/ Lewis-as-himself, Lewis-as-himself/Berle-as-bellboy, Lewis-as-Stanley/ Berle-as-bellboy. It's like the working out of a mathematical problem on a blackboard (see fig. 3). This is the kind of formal problem that increasingly concerns Lewis: for example, the problem of *how* to tell a joke, how to formalize and arrange it. Lewis writes in *The Total Film-Maker,* "In my case there are thirty ways to show a joke—insert it, cut to it, refer to it, punch it, lay back, double-cut! But why, and how?" (128).

The block is not a part through which the themes of the whole continue to move, receiving a development that is only relatively independent of the whole. The block is a collision of bodies and the space-time that contains them, a set of poses or actions ("hanging here and groping there") that are present with each other but that remain apart instead of complementing or embracing each other. In *The Ladies Man,* while Katie, with whom he has crossed paths by chance, rattles on in praise of his work ("You are just living proof that good people are good things to be"), Herbert, oblivious, recites the instructions he has just received from the visiting Gainsborough (Buddy Lester). The meeting of Herbert and Katie will have been a nonmeeting: they

Figure 3. *The Bellboy:* Jerry Lewis as
Jerry Lewis, Milton Berle as a bellboy.

share the same space, as defined by Lewis's mise-en-scène; nothing passes between them; they separate.

Because it is only a single unit, without hierarchies, the block frees the isolatedness of the gestures or actions it contains and lets them exist for themselves, without subordinating them to a narrative logic. In the Miss Cartilage sequence of *The Ladies Man,* Herbert's action exists next to Miss Cartilage's action and next to the action of Harry James and his orchestra, who are magically present in Miss Cartilage's vast suite. The juxtaposition of these actions constitutes a single block. The dance scene in *Three on a Couch* is a block of back-and-forth lateral movement, set to music, a single drifting-out and -back.

The block tendency in Lewis's work reaches its full development in *The Family Jewels:* the episode and the anecdote *for themselves* predominate over the plot; or rather, the plot merely justifies the episodes. Since each block has a different main character, the discontinuity of the film is greater than usual with Lewis. What matters most is movement for its own sake as a formal requirement of the film. Another formal requirement is met by Willard summoning all the uncles at Donna's moment of crisis—although they fail to arrive and are of no help in rescuing her. The chance convergence of Willard, the marchers, and Skylock and Matson (Sebastian Cabot) at Bugsy's waterfront hideout represents not so much a surrealist vindication of chance as the completion of a filmic structure that is called into play by no other power than the sheer love of watching lines converge.

The Performance of Identity

Not only scenes but people, too, can be blocks. In *Three on a Couch,* each of the three target women is a block of preferences and weaknesses to which Chris adapts himself to become the male ideal. In *Which Way to the Front?,* Kesselring is a block of traits that Byers tries to imitate. In *Hardly Working,* each of Bo's jobs is a block of challenges in dealing with the physical universe.

This mode of characterization represents Lewis's rebellion against the structures of the American feature-length film. In the Martin and Lewis films and in his early solo efforts, Lewis's characters, though freakish in their behavior and socially inadequate, stay reined in by conventional narratives that focus on their relationships with the characters played by Martin, fathers or father figures (such as Eddie Mayehoff's dominating ex–football star in *That's My Boy*), women as love interests, and children. However aggressively his performance pushes against the narrative frames, Lewis's characters function in their service.

Stanley in *The Bellboy* has no responsibilities to such a structure, and this liberation, reflected in the film's episodic construction, deeply affects the conception of the character. Stanley has no past (compare the flashback sequences that detail the Lewis character's back story in, for example, Taurog's *The Caddy* [1953]). He has no goals other than the immediate ones defined by the tasks he is assigned. He has no close male friend, no female love object, no parental figures (except, perhaps, the hotel manager [Alex Gerry], but their interactions are insignificant until the final scene). Nothing defines Stanley except his functioning in small, discrete, bounded situations in which his relationships are usually with objects (the engine he removes from the Volkswagen, the pair of pants he presses too thoroughly, the elevator that doesn't come, the chairs he sets up in the ballroom, the airplane he borrows). Stanley exists completely within the separate blocks of the film.

The comic performer, in Lewis's view, forms "an erratic pattern" that encompasses characters who are, in fact, different. Lewis explains: "Chaplin was both the *shlemiel* and the *shlimazel*. He was the guy who spilled the drinks—the *shlemiel*—and the guy who had the drinks spilled on him—the *shlimazel*. In his shadings of comedy, and they were like a rainbow, he also played a combination of *shlemiel-shlimazel*. . . . My Idiot character plays both the *shlemiel* and the *shlimazel*, at times the inter-mix. I'm always conscious of the three factors—done to, doing to self, and doing to someone else by accident or design—while playing him, but they are not in acute focus. They swim in and out at any given moment" (Lewis, *Total Film-Maker* 198). The Lewisian person is not merely inconsistent, he is discontinuous. In *The Ladies Man,* Herbert in the highchair as Katie feeds him is self-assertive and aggressive, unlike in other scenes. In the restaurant where he takes Ellen (Ina Balin) in *The Patsy,* the gentle and inept Stanley Belt, put on the defensive when the headwaiter (Fritz Feld) kisses Ellen's hand, suddenly breaks into Buddy Love voice and attitude. Stanley's parody of social niceness at the cocktail party, letting loose with an unexpected show-biz "sweetie," implies a consciousness of modes of speech that the character has not previously demonstrated and that his characterization does not account for. At the end of *The Errand Boy,* Morty suddenly acquires a new vocal timbre and a new vocabulary ("Love ya"). In *Three on a Couch,* the seemingly involuntary verbal reactions elicited from Chris when a line of female models files past him in a clothing store involve a mixing of voices explicable neither in terms of Chris's psychology nor in terms of his attempt to make his "Ringo Raintree" disguise plausible, as he slips out of his "Western" accent into other Lewisian vocal mannerisms.

Lewis as director doesn't thematize these changes or recuperate them within the kind of structure that declares that the apparent inconsistencies are intended as a complex characterization and that they will be (and therefore already are in advance) resolved somehow. Lewis refuses to resolve. An apparent exception is the end of *The Nutty Professor,* which implies the possibility for Kelp and Love to become synthesized. But synthesis never occurs: there is nothing but conflict and reversal (this is clearer at the end of *The Errand Boy,* in which Morty and his double confront each other: they shake hands and are in some sense united, but they remain two different people).

In the Magnolia scene in *The Errand Boy,* Morty suddenly becomes able to give a naturalistic, psychological explanation for his constant screwing up: "It's just that I've been so delighted with working here that I didn't think half of the time." In *The Big Mouth,* the narrator speculates on Clamson's motives in trying to get into the Hilton Inn and comes up with three possibilities: the diamonds, frustration at not being able to get anybody to listen to him, and interest in Suzie. In both films, the explanation is merely a hypothesis, an optional way of understanding the character. This is also true in *The Nutty Professor:* the hypothesis that would explain the behavior of Love, and that of Kelp, merely exists in the ideational space of the narrative; it doesn't resolve the mysteries of the film.

In Lewis's films, the separate blocks of identity that constitute his characters are unified, if at all, only by Lewis himself: as a body, as a famous star, as a complex image. Chaplin said, in response to critics of his camera style, "I don't need interesting camera angles. *I* am interesting." Though his own work with the camera is often spectacularly interesting, Lewis could say the same: he makes himself the justification, the substance of the film. (There are exceptions, especially *One More Time*, in which Lewis does not appear, and *The Big Mouth* and *Which Way to the Front?*, in which he deliberately foregrounds, for parts of the film, other comedians, such as Charlie Callas in the former and Jan Murray and Steve Franken in the latter—a strategy that can be traced back to *The Bellboy*, with the disruptive and hilarious nightclub performance of the Las Vegas stage act the Novelites.)

Lewis refers explicitly to his own career and his status as a star in *The Bellboy, The Errand Boy,* and *The Patsy* (he began doing this as early as *The Caddy*). In a key section of *The Bellboy,* Lewis appears as himself—a famous, powerful star surrounded and encumbered by a large entourage. In *The Errand Boy,* the self-reference takes the form of a personal myth, that of the movie fan from New Jersey who goes to Hollywood to be close to the source of his dreams, only to find them farther away than ever. Morty's story differs in a crucial respect from Lewis's: like Malcolm Smith (Lewis) in Tashlin's *Hollywood or Bust,* Morty made the trip to Hollywood on his own initiative, as an unknown; when Lewis went to Hollywood, he was already a star. Stanley Belt's trajectory in *The Patsy* can also be seen as a mythologizing of Lewis's career in that Stanley, too, rises from a low social position and a career characterized by mishaps to become a star (the film even contains an aborted reference to Lewis's own record act: to fill time during his desultory stand-up debut at the Copa Café, Stanley brings a portable phonograph on stage, intending to mouth the lyrics to his own hit record, but is unable to make the machine work). Stanley's ability to triumph without his team of experienced show-business professionals— who, after "discovering" him and masterminding his rise to stardom, abandon him on the critical night of his guest appearance on *The Ed Sullivan Show*—can be read as an oblique version of Lewis's success at obtaining control over his career by functioning as writer, director, and producer. At the end of the film, Lewis emerges, after the apparent accidental death of the character he is playing, in his own persona as director and star (making it explicit that the whole narrative, in which Stanley is called on to substitute for an already dead star, is a self-reflexive fantasy in which Lewis reinvents himself and starts over from the beginning). *The Patsy* contains several more incidental self-references: during the splendidly stylized street scenes of Ellen trying to get in touch with Stanley before he receives the kiss-off letter from his staff, we see a *Who's Minding the*

Store? poster (just as in *The Disorderly Orderly* there appears an ad for *The Patsy*); even Stanley's entrance line ("The bellboy") can be heard as a reference to the title of Lewis's first directed film.

In his other films, Lewis incorporates self-referential notations and lines and situations that resonate with his own biography. In *The Big Mouth,* the joy of the gangster Thor (Harold J. Stone) at learning of the supposed death of Valentine (the gangster played by Lewis) can be heard as a comment on the animus against Lewis expressed by many critics. In the same film, the hotel manager and other characters harbor an irrational, excessive hatred of Lewis. As early as *The Bellboy,* Lewis shows his consciousness of the difficulty of his position in American popular culture: standing with his boss in front of the hotel, waiting for the arrival of a famous star, a hotel employee apologizes for his initial outburst of enthusiasm ("And it's Jerry Lewis!") by saying deprecatingly, "Our mother used to take me to see him when I was a kid." (Part of the joke is that the man looks old enough to have been in college before Lewis was born.) Byers's lament at the beginning of *Which Way to the Front?* also strikes an autobiographical note: "I have nothing to look forward to, nothing but what I've already done."

Lewis brings himself—his history, his personality, his public image and its vicissitudes—into *Hardly Working* and *Cracking Up* with an explicitness that is highly audacious even for him. *Hardly Working* begins with an opening montage of greatest hits from *Cinderfella, The Errand Boy, Who's Minding the Store?,* and other Lewis triumphs. This sequence establishes that the hero of *Hardly Working,* Bo Hooper, is fundamentally Jerry Lewis himself. The film relocates the star, playing an aging clown who is suddenly thrown out of work, in a time that threatens him with obsolescence and irrelevance (see fig. 4). In *Cracking Up* (like the beginning of *Hardly Working,* a reintroduction to Lewis), the Lewis character's response to his felt untimeliness is to attempt suicide. The suicide motif seems to call out to be read as an autobiographical allusion to Lewis's own suicide impulse (which he later revealed publicly). Unlike *Hardly Working, Cracking Up* proposes no past glories to heighten a contrast with the ignoble present. Still, Lewis's past swarms behind the film. The scene in *Cracking Up* with Milton Berle in drag as a female patient of Dr. Pletchick repeats the scene of Stanley waiting outside a row of phone booths in *The Bellboy:* again, the Lewis character hears a woman's voice saying things that arouse his amatory interest, but the person who emerges turns out to be a man. *Cracking Up* repeats a motif of the Lewis character's negative relationship with art objects, which gives rise to a series of surrealistic gags, as in *The Bellboy* (the sculpture whose still-soft clay Stanley inadvertently reshapes) and *The Errand Boy* (the Samson figure between two pillars, framed portrait-like in the cafeteria, who is actually three-dimensional and is holding together structural materials, and whom Morty causes to fall by pulling a thread). The cab driver running after a moving car in *The Family Jewels* and the cheapjack airline in the same film reappear in *Cracking Up*.

Hardly Working and *Cracking Up* are apologies for the life of a misfit, dropout manifestos. For Lewis in these late films, it is a question of reconquering territory that has already been taken and abandoned. Both films dramatize the regaining of confidence in spatial terms as a regaining of position and of territory. In *Cracking Up*, Warren marks a temporary triumph over his klutziness by managing to walk across the floor of his psychiatrist's office toward the doctor's open arms. At the

Figure 4. Bo (Jerry Lewis) faces an uncertain future in *Hardly Working*.

end of the film, Warren walks again—across the street to two women he successfully chats up.

In what is only apparently a paradox, Lewis's ubiquity as a performer in his films goes along with a radical questioning of individuality and identity. In the mirror scene in Sy Devore's clothing shop in *The Patsy*, when the tracking camera shows George Raft in a hitherto unrevealed panel of the mirror, Stanley has so little sense of his own identity that he mistakes Raft's reflection for his own. The confusion of person and cutout in *The Bellboy*—Stanley trying to deliver a message to the cutout—is eloquent. In the spectacular society that Lewis depicts so scathingly, a person counts for so little and has an identity so evanescent that a photograph or a mirror image might be mistaken for the person him- or herself. It is a world of flattened, manufactured images, a show-business world—created by and for the business of showing—in which people are always signs of themselves.

Identity in Lewis is always performed; there is no private self, and an audience is always present, often explicitly. In *The Ladies Man*, Herbert refuses to believe George Raft's claim of who he is and demands that he prove his identity by, in effect, playing Raft. (It's revealing that both of Raft's appearances in Lewis's films involve a questioning of identity. Lewis uses Raft as an ideal masculine image to show that the image is not "only" an image but *first and foremost* an image, one that the Lewis character and George Raft himself have trouble living up to.) Lewis's direction of actors insists on an exaggeration that implies an awareness of an audience, suggesting that his characters (like those of John Cassavetes) are constantly involved in performances of themselves. The social world of Lewis's films is luxuriantly stylized: Helen Traubel as the fulsome boarding-house proprietor Mrs. Wellenmelon in *The Ladies Man*, Bob Clayton as the smooth bell captain in *The Bellboy*, the Jewish bellboys (and dog-track aficionados) in *The Bellboy*, Howard McNear as the groveling Mr. Sneak in *The Errand Boy*, the overplaying actors in the parody "movie" scenes of *The Errand Boy*. James Best's performance as Chris's friend Ben introduces a hectic and inflamed atmosphere into *Three on a Couch*. Irritation and frustration are constant in Lewis's universe, giving rise to a generalized aggression that frequently takes the Lewis character as its target: for example, the

Figure 5. Jerry Lewis and Del Moore
in *The Big Mouth*.

vehemence of Neil Hamilton's lawyer in *The Family Jewels* and the hyperbolic rage of the hotel manager in *The Big Mouth* (see fig. 5).

The Big Mouth showcases Clamson's reactions to the various grotesques who confront him and the absurd situations in which he finds himself. His attempt to transpose his encounters with the criminals into the register of ordinary social interaction, of ordinary display of self, takes him through various stages of self-creation. Before his encounter with Valentine, his double, it's as if he has forgotten himself or been in hiding: he has to relearn and reinvent himself, to become himself again (or for the first time). The question for him is, How to be? Answering this question, his gestures and actions are immediate, quick, and simple. To the deliberately smooth, Everyman-like manner Lewis adopts as actor for the moments when Clamson appears as himself, Lewis as director contrasts a range of grotesques: Thor roaring at his three subordinates, the transformations they undergo after encountering Clamson (whom they believe to be the resurrected Valentine), the irrational murderous vengefulness of the hotel manager. While Clamson becomes more and more simple and direct, the other characters (except Suzie, his ally) fall prey to a fatality for extremity and exaggeration. What Clamson encounters in other people is exemplified in an extreme way by the figure of the lunatic who claims to be the chief of the FBI: reckless solipsism and a fixation on the imaginary self.

"Be somebody—be *anybody.*" This exhortation, spoken (and printed on a card) near the end of *The Nutty Professor* by Kelp's milquetoast father (Howard Morris) after his transformation into a dominating huckster, is carried out by Chris Pride in *Three on a Couch,* whose status as an established artist marks Lewis's own emergence in a "mature" role (perhaps we should say "majoritarian," in the Deleuze-Guattari senses of normative, dominant, and colonizing): he no longer plays the put-upon, humiliated misfit (though not for the first time in his career: already we have seen Lewis-as-star in *The Bellboy,* Morty-as-star at the end of *The Errand Boy,* and Stanley-as-star at the end of *The Patsy;* we've seen Buddy Love and Uncle Everett). Unlike Kelp in *The Nutty Professor,* Chris apparently has no internal difficulty to overcome: his difficulty is presented as something outside him. But this external difficulty, through his manner of opposing it, reveals the cracks within himself, and he is progressively forced to abandon his majoritarian position.

Three on a Couch is thus the inverse of *The Nutty Professor,* in which Kelp seeks to improve his self-image through chemistry. In *Three on a Couch,* the man who has made it and who has all kinds of success ("I'm just completely secure," Chris tells Elizabeth early in the film) is compelled to go back down the ladder, to reinvent himself in more limited and grotesque forms. Chris's varied characterizations all deviate from the standard that he himself represents. They are less universal than he is: they are aficionados (of physical fitness, rodeo, and entomology), one is a woman (and thus deviant or defective within the phallocentric world the film depicts—and criticizes), and they have regional accents. This process is a metaphor for Lewis's basic conception of comedy, as he stated it in his interview with me: "In order to make your audience laugh, you have to dramatically change who you are. I won't trip over that piece of wood on the stage if it's me walking there. But Jerry will, or Stanley, or the Idiot, or whatever we call him in that moment. He *has* to trip over it. Now, he has to turn into something that isn't truly him, so we're taking a piece of vanity and rubbing it out, a little ego, burying it, sandpapering all that down, and bringing up all of the gargoyles. . . . There's nothing more dramatic than that moment. . . . Because I have to call on something that's not what I want to be at that moment. I want to be there with my girl or my wife watching some other schmuck make a fool of himself. But I never ever thought of what I did as demeaning. What I thought of it was: other than me at that moment."

Chris calculates each of his impersonations to appeal to one of Elizabeth's three patients, on the basis of what he knows about their interests, backgrounds, and case histories. Beyond the traits he assumes to attract the women (Rutherford has only to be interested in zoology, to be shy with women, and to speak with a southern accent; Ringo has only to be a westerner; Warren has only to be athletic), the content of the characterization is free. Why, to attract Mary Lou (Leslie Parrish), does Chris become the prissy Rutherford (and, first, Rutherford's devoted sister, Heather) rather than some other character? (A similar question could be asked about *Cracking Up.* The bank robber, the country sheriff: what are these persons?) The first answer is: he has to be *somebody.* Nobody can be just an abstract person, a nonentity (though Clamson in *The Big Mouth* comes close). Since we have to be somebody, the Lewis character seems to say, let's be somebody special.

Related to this imperative is Kelp's realization, in *The Nutty Professor,* that "you might as well like yourself." Kelp's conclusion has yet to be corrected by the film, and, though Lewis seems to make it as difficult as possible to separate his own authorial voice from Kelp's at this point (with Kelp addressing the silent onscreen audience at the prom), we should resist the temptation to believe that Kelp is here delivering the film's definitive "message." The correction comes in the final sequence, with the reappearance of Kelp's parents and the snake-oil-salesman's pitch of Kelp's father. In light of the father's speech, we might amend Kelp's message at the prom: go ahead and like yourself, and why not, since you are, in essence, "anybody." All identities are roles that can be purchased, altered, borrowed (Lewis shows that Kelp, under the guidance of Stella [Stella Stevens], has already begun to "correct" his appearance, with braces on his teeth and product in his hair). I can be you, and you can be me—the principle of equivalence or exchange that the psychiatrist and his patient obey at the end of *Cracking Up.*

The person is optional and unreal in Lewis's films, nothing more than a set of possibilities or a collection of stereotypes (as in *Cracking Up*). Lewis makes the invention of a character an explicit theme when, in *Which Way to the Front?*, the members of Byers's team give their various impressions of Kesselring's walk, which each man endows with imaginary eccentricities seemingly borrowed from his own ideal self-image. A character is always a collection of traits, such as the glasses, voice, hairstyle, and clothes of the second Clamson (*The Big Mouth*) and the kabuki wig, white face makeup (reduction to zero), and kimono he dons in an attempt to hide in plain sight from his pursuers. In *The Big Mouth*, the basis to which all these changes are applied is a blank: the bookkeeper Clamson, neither ridiculous nor admirable, not anything much at all apart from his function and his vacation-time hobby, just as Stanley in *The Bellboy* defines himself entirely by his work and his relation to it. None of Lewis's other characters are much more than that (which makes them no less human; rather the contrary).

The Lewis character has an infinite receptive capacity; he is hypersensitive and ready to incorporate anything felt, believed, or projected by another person. Gilles Deleuze writes of Lewis, "Everything resonates in his head and in his soul" (88). In a classic scene in *The Nutty Professor*, the various sounds in the classroom, magnified, resonate within Kelp. In *Hardly Working*, Bo takes into himself and emits Balling's voice, laboriously repeating his pedantic instructions. In *The Errand Boy*, Morty introjects the names Babewosentall and Wabenlottnee (but discharges them differently). The Lewis character is always a receiver (a theme that is most fully developed in Tashlin's *The Disorderly Orderly*, in which Jerome's "sympathy pains" mimic his patients' symptoms), though he is often a "carrier," too (of mail, as in *The Ladies Man, The Errand Boy*, and *Hardly Working*). He is always potentially anybody and always takes into himself, acts out, and extends the possibilities he encounters in other people.

As Jean-Louis Comolli points out, however, "Why so many doubles thrown to the four winds of the screen, if not in order *not* to be them?" (Comolli 54). The multiplication of Lewis's selves—his caricatures of a studio head, a director, and a writer in the trailer for *The Bellboy* (depicting filmmaking as discontinuity and fragmentation of identity); his seven roles in *The Family Jewels;* and Chris's disguises in *Three on a Couch* provide striking examples—is a form of negation, just as Morty's mimicry of his bosses in *The Errand Boy* is a way of rejecting the over-powerful paternal authority they represent. Moreover, the multiplication of Lewises in his films, rather than being merely narcissistic, is only one form of a general multiplicity that explodes across the screen (in, for example, the proliferation of women in the morning sequence of *The Ladies Man*).

It's hard to deny that Lewis's work is, nevertheless, devoted to a cult of the self (which partly accounts for the strong negative reactions he has inspired in many). His work is a multidimensional and self-contradictory staging of selfhood: an artist's documentation and consideration of his own existence. In this connection, *The Patsy* and *Cracking Up* are especially interesting as the two Lewis films in which he directly confronts the possibility of his own character's death (as he does, more obliquely, in *The Family Jewels* and *The Big Mouth*): the films try to define and preserve selfhood even as they play with its disappearance, only to end up acknowledging the fictional and optional nature of selfhood and (like *Three on a Couch*) the untenability of any standard of "success." The possibility that identity and individuality could be eradicated or annulled always lies underneath the dazzling variety of Lewis's playful constructions of identity: the opening of *Hardly Working* owes its melancholy to Bo's sudden painful realization that his identity as a clown has been cancelled, and the rest of the film will detail (though obscurely and brokenly) his progress toward resuming it.

A real discontinuity in Lewis's biography—one day he was a nobody, and the next day he was a star—constantly remains within his grasp or, rather, constantly threatens him, making him insecure in his success ("I see the stage suddenly turn to sawdust, my tux change to a tramp's outfit, and I feel as though people are looking at me like I'm some kind of freak in a sideshow" [Lewis and Gluck 290]). Lewis's insistence on representing this insecurity and facing it directly makes *The Nutty Professor* deeply painful, just as *The Big Mouth* is so lacerating and uncomfortable because it exposes the arbitrariness of any decision to be any person whatever.

The role is independent from the person playing it, but at the time of the performance the person exists only through the role. In *The Family Jewels*, "Uncle Everett," the egocentric clown who is filled with loathing for his audience and his fellow performers, can be played by Everett himself and, at the end of the film, by Willard. In *Which Way to the*

Front?, Kesselring can be played by himself and by Byers. The role is a block of identity that different agents can activate at different times. The arbitrariness of the person is related to the arbitrariness of the film's premise: when the two coincide, as in *The Errand Boy* and *The Patsy*, we reach the quintessence of Lewisian cinema.

Where does life end and performance begin? *The Errand Boy* and *The Patsy* propose a continuity between the two. The famed columnist Hedda Hopper tells Stanley's handlers in *The Patsy:* "You've come across somebody who hasn't yet learned to be phony. He felt something, and he said it, which was real and honest. And now if you apply that to his performance, you've got a great success." In *The Errand Boy,* Morty's attempts to cope with a spouting champagne bottle are captured on film, and his "performance" is pronounced hilarious by three experts. One of them (Robert Ivers) is a New York director (whose declamatory style is itself Method-like, "New York") who defines acting in this way: "Anyone in the world would give anything to do a performance. Because performing is nothing more than a form of expression. But not anyone is capable of expressing themselves openly and freely. And therefore only a few, only a very few are chosen. Chosen to communicate and express for the millions that either can't, don't know how, or would never get the opportunity to do so. And those few that are chosen are called actors. But they're still people. And I might add, a very special kind of people." This communicative power has a special priority and purity for Lewis. It can cut through the apparatus of mass media and render irrelevant the system (and the class) of technocrats and experts who organize perception. At the beginning of *The Patsy,* Lewis is careful to emphasize that the dead comedian Wally Brandford taught his handlers most of what they know about show business.

Near the end of *The Patsy,* Stanley Belt appears on the *Ed Sullivan Show* in a skit that, ostensibly, he has improvised, or at any rate created himself (since we are told that he has not used any of the material that Chic [Phil Harris] wrote for him), and his performance is declared a great success.[3] The sequence was originally intended as a flashback to Stanley's previous experience, which he relates to Ellen. It was switched to its final position in the film when the routine Lewis had written for the *Ed Sullivan Show* sequence—Stanley undergoing a series of mishaps on the set of a car commercial—turned out not to work. The logic of the rejected car-commercial sequence, which might have been more intelligible than the sequence that appears in the film, is the same as that of the scene with the champagne bottle in *The Errand Boy:* the Lewis character's revelation of performance "skill" emerges unintentionally (this logic appears earlier in *The Patsy,* in the cocktail-party scene with Hedda Hopper). The logic of the "premiere" sequence in the final film is ambivalent: either we assume that Stanley has, without his handlers' knowledge, taken over their functions by writing, rehearsing, and staging his own skit with the *Ed Sullivan Show's* actors and crew, or we read the scene as a fantasy—an option that may appear more insistent if we reflect on the similarities between this scene (in which the down-at-heel Lewis figure inventively transforms himself into a toff in evening dress to crash a movie premiere) and the classic ballroom scene in Tashlin's *Cinderfella.*[4] Both are scenes of metamorphosis, involving the revelation of a performance mastery that is also the revelation of a personality, an assumed identity that may be taken as more real than the real identity.

In Lewis's films, the assumption of identity takes the metaphorical form of the performance of a job. Work is a double determination: on the one hand, a person's possibilities need to be fixed and defined (which is to say, the indeterminateness of these possibilities needs to be denied); on the other hand, the worker, in being given a task, comes to feel that he or she has a role and a place. In *The Ladies Man,* work is defined as giving someone things to do so he or she will feel needed. The ostensible product of the labor has marginal value; the main value lies in the feelings of participation and necessity that are its by-products. (Dana Polan writes that in "Lewis's films, . . . work [is] not really imagined as alienation after all" [Polan, "Working Hard" 214].) Byers's project in *Which Way to the Front?,* arising out of the need to overcome the army's crushing and disorienting rejection, is a labor of this type: that Byers and his band of volunteers form a functioning unit that helps the Allies win World War II is secondary: the emphasis throughout is on the arbitrary exercise of Byers's power of performance in situations in which he finds himself (disguised as Kesselring) in the central role.

The abstract requirement for the new position of studio spy, as stated by Mr. Paramutual (Brian Donlevy) in *The Errand Boy:* someone who is anybody, whom nobody knows, who doesn't care about his own problems or anybody else's, who has no interest in money. Morty appears magically to fulfill these requirements, just as, in *The Nutty Professor*, Love appears magically to fulfill the requirements that Kelp has internalized (from their dissemination in culture) for an ideal masculine image. It is as if Morty's presence and even his existence were summoned up by the studio executive's words. All employees are nonpersons who come into being and assume a definite form only by entering the position, the role, the job. Just as Chris Pride in *Three on a Couch* divides into different people to carry out his plan—becoming, as he does so, more vivid and more real—Bo in *Hardly Working* divides into different people and becomes, in turn, each of his jobs.

The Lewis characters' peculiar relationships with money highlight the significance of the job in their world. The scene in *The Patsy* in which Stanley, taking Ellen to a fancy restaurant, demonstrates his unfamiliarity with tipping etiquette by giving lavish tips to each member of a long succession of service personnel, is a masterpiece of awkwardness (see fig. 6). In this scene, Lewis plays on an aporia of the quantification of humanity in money: it is abusive to reduce a person to an amount of money, yet service providers must be paid something. Stanley's error is to attempt to compensate for the dehumanization inherent in paying someone a wage by indefinitely inflating the wage—an error that is

Figure 6. The tipping scene in *The Patsy:*
Jerry Lewis and Ina Balin.

acutely embarrassing for everyone because it reveals the contradiction within the system.

Only with *Three on a Couch* does the Lewis character for the first time acquire the competence to control money and deal in specific quantities of it. Told that his prize amounts to the equivalent in French francs of "ten thousand dollars, give or take," Chris replies, "You give, I'll take"—reversing Stanley's procedure in *The Patsy*. In *Which Way to the Front?*, Byers has so much money that possession is no longer a challenge to him, and he secures the participation of his wavering recruits by promising them one hundred thousand dollars each at the completion of their mission.

Money is less decisive than the job in securing identity (though money is the power that also threatens to reveal the illusory nature of the identity thus secured). Asked by his sister (Susan Oliver) what he really wants, Bo replies in terms that recall Kelp's father's exhortation at the end of *The Nutty Professor* and Morty's account of himself to Magnolia in *The Errand Boy:* "I want what I never realized I wanted. To be somebody. Not just anybody, but somebody. With a direction and a purpose. For as long as I can remember, I thought I was satisfied with this job, that job, any job. As long as I had three squares a day and a place to put my head. But I think it's about time I dug some roots for myself. With a steady job and steady money." This speech, with its critical distinguishing of "somebody" from "anybody," can be heard as a riposte to Kelp's father at the end of *The Nutty Professor.* It propounds an ideological confusion—of personal identity with a job—that *Hardly Working* finally rejects, even though Bo utters the speech in apparent sincerity, and his adoring sister takes it as proof of his new maturity. The film finally denounces the steady job, and the direction and the purpose it confers, as denying human possibilities, whereas Bo's vocation of clown puts him in contact with the indeterminateness of these possibilities. The end of *Hardly Working* recalls that of *The Family Jewels:* the protagonist turns his back on society and sets out with his loved one (like the Tramp and the girl at the end of Chaplin's *Modern Times* [1936]) toward an uncertain future. Like *The Family Jewels, Hardly Working* is an apparently sentimental and conformist film that discloses a deep distrust of the dominant values of its society.

Saying No to No

In *The Errand Boy,* Morty stumbles into a group of suits of armor that first appear to be empty costumes propped against a wall but that, after he knocks them over, prove to be filled by human wearers who slowly rouse themselves and struggle to get up from the ground. This scene, like the later one in which Morty is mistaken for a prop dummy, invokes the frightening uncertainty of the mannequin, the instability of the line separating the animate and the inanimate, the susceptibility of the human individual to be replaced by a double. In a flashback sequence in *Cracking Up,* a dummy is accidentally liberated from prison in place of Warren Nefron's hapless French ancestor (played by Lewis). In Tashlin's *Hollywood or Bust,* Steve (Dean Martin) and Malcolm (Lewis) gain access to a movie studio by pretending to be, respectively, a prop man and a dummy (questioned by a suspicious guard, Steve assures him, "That's a real dummy"). In a resonant gag in Tashlin's *The Disorderly Orderly,* Jerome (Lewis), out for a walk on the hospital lawn with a patient encased completely in a plaster body-cast, inattentively leaves him standing on the edge of a hill for a moment, only for the mummy to collapse, roll down the hill, and shatter against a tree. When Jerome reaches the wreckage, he finds the plaster pieces to be hollow.

The mannequin is an extreme form of a figure that appears often in Lewis's films: the unresponsive partner. Typically, this person remains stone-faced before the antics of the Lewis character, like Henry Silva's stepbrother Maximilian in Tashlin's *Cinderfella*, whose cigarette Lewis's Fella repeatedly tries to light with destructive results. Since the unresponsive partner represents a development of the founding duality of the Martin and Lewis partnership—in Lewis's words, "a handsome man and a monkey"—a duality that has remained important to Lewis's work since the breakup of the comedy team, it is worthwhile to analyze that duality here.

The origins of the act lay in Lewis's unrehearsed interruption of Martin's nightclub performance (Lewis and Kaplan 22). Perhaps the inaugural duality of the team, more basic than handsomeness/simianness, lies here: continuity versus rupture. During one of their first shows together, Lewis shut off all the lights in the nightclub while Martin was singing "Pennies from Heaven," befuddling the musicians and making them stop playing. "[A]nd Dean—of course!—never hesitated for a second. . . . Going on with his number (even a capella) was a matter of pride for him." Improvising a small spotlight by holding his Zippo lighter close to his face, Martin "finished his song in the mellow flicker of its flame just as though nothing at all had happened" (Lewis and Kaplan 328). Always, it's a question of rhythm. Commenting on his partner's "magical" sense of timing, Lewis exults: "I can't tell you what this looks like to somebody whose life is predicated on rhythm" (Lewis and Kaplan 42).

Martin's smooth imperturbability in the presence of chaos made him a perfect foil for Lewis. "Some part of [Martin] was always standing back, making fun of what he did," Lewis writes (Lewis and Kaplan 36). The singer's background predisposed him to this even detachment. Martin's Italian immigrant parents, according to Lewis, brought him up with a coldness and harshness that made young Dino feel lonely and unloved (feelings he shared with the young Lewis, though for different reasons) and that left him with a fundamental sense of solitude and a refusal to betray emotion—even, Lewis believed, to the point of being unable to feel his own pain (Lewis and Kaplan 275). Though "he maintained that distance from everybody except me," in Lewis's words, so that the two men established a "closeness [that] worked for us, bonding us in the way the audiences loved" (Lewis and Kaplan 104), that distance also set him apart from Lewis and gave the team what Andrew Sarris called "a marvelous tension" (243).

According to Sarris, this tension was not preserved in Martin and Lewis's movies (243). Perhaps it would be more accurate to say that though tension, and sometimes even hostility, between the partners *does* come through quite sharply in the films (especially such late ones as Taurog's *You're Never Too Young* [1955] and Tashlin's *Hollywood or Bust*, during the making of which the two stars, off-camera, were not on speaking terms), what sometimes fails to come through, or comes through to a lesser degree, is the element that made the tension "marvelous": their compensating closeness. Frank Krutnik sums up the chemistry between Martin and Lewis as "a conflictual harmony that encompasses closeness and distance, tenderness and hostility, euphoria and ambivalence" (Krutnik, "Sex and Slapstick" 113). The special performance relationship Martin and Lewis enjoyed comes across less directly in their films than in their appearances as regular guest hosts of the *Colgate Comedy Hour* television series, in which, as Scott Bukatman notes, "Martin reveals an ability to follow and respond to Lewis, providing a measure of control while sharing in the delights of comic anarchy" (190).

In his solo and especially his self-directed films, Lewis breaks up, modifies, reinvents, and recasts various aspects of the complex structural role Martin played in relation to him. The masterful, well-liked Martin returns in the "double" figure played by Lewis himself in his own films: one who attains a social success that is denied his alter ego (who is in some cases his previous self): "Jerry Lewis" in *The Bellboy,* Morty as star at the end of *The Errand Boy,* Buddy Love in *The Nutty Professor,* the vindicated and newly self-confident Stanley (shortly to metamorphose into director/star Jerry Lewis) at the end of *The Patsy,* the self-assured Warren at the end of *Cracking Up.* (The six uncles in *The Family Jewels* are all parodies of the socially successful male figure: though they have achieved some degree of success and independence, they are clearly inept in their professions.) Another aspect of Martin—the sponsor or supporter of the Lewis character, linking him to mainstream society— reemerges as the friend, counselor, helper, or expert incarnated by such figures as Ben in *Three on a Couch,* the Peter Lawford character in *Hook, Line, and Sinker* (credited to George Marshall but produced by Lewis and bearing, in parts, his stylistic signature [see Lewis, *Total Film-Maker* 33 and Benayoun 313–14]), and the psychiatrist in *Cracking Up.* Of these, Ben in *Three on a Couch* is the most interesting case: if he is vestigially Martin-like in conspiring with and legitimizing the Lewis figure (in *Living It Up,* for example, Martin plays the physician who helps the Lewis character maintain the fiction that he is dying of an incurable disease) and establishing a link between the Lewis figure and the larger society, he is a Martin become uncomplainingly subservient to his partner's personality and designs. As played by James Best, Ben, unlike Martin, has little self-control and is not cool: repeatedly, he makes so obvious his panicked reaction to the emergence of possible setbacks to their scheme that Chris has to enjoin him to relax.

Chris Pepper in *One More Time* is another interesting variation on the "friend" character: in this film, it is the relatively well-adjusted, well-socialized, Martinesque male (whose normative function is also racialized, since Chris is white, while Charlie is black) who splits into two roles (Chris and his twin brother, Sydney). The film also expands on the theme of betrayal—present in several Martin and Lewis films—in the *Hound of the Baskervilles*-esque plot element of Chris's failure to let Charlie in on his plan to disguise himself and even allowing Charlie to believe that he is dead, while a certain irony is also present in Charlie's delay in recognizing Chris. Betrayal is also a key element in *The Patsy, Hook, Line, and Sinker,* and the unreleased *The Day the Clown Cried.* Most crucially, Martin's distance and his refusal to be moved are embodied in unresponsive-partner figures like Maximilian in *Cinderfella,* the bell captain in *The Bellboy,* and Dr. Warfield (Del Moore) in *The Nutty Professor*—surrogate older brothers or fathers whom the Lewis character desperately and ineptly tries to please, only to be met with a mask of disapproval or indifference. In other films, the figure of the unresponsive partner is more generalized. Lewis breaks down the great elevator sequence of *The Errand Boy* into a series of two-shot confrontations in which Morty is nose-to-nose with another person who refuses to acknowledge him. In the early recruiting-office sequence of *Which Way to the Front?,* Lewis cuts between Byers's out-of-control babbling (in response to the word "rejection") and the amazed reactions of his fellow 4-Fs. On his first appearance in *The Patsy,* Stanley, presenting himself at the door of the Brandford staff's suite with an ice bucket and a tray of glasses, keeps up, in the face of the others' silence, a commentary on what he has just done, what he is now doing, and what he could do next. "You see when I, uh, I had it, my, all my clothes were wet, so I changed my clothes, because when I w—, that's why I was long. Should I p-put, or not? Just stand? I'll close the door. I'll—I'll—the key ring is caught in the, uh, door, but I'll get the—I can rinse all of these out. . . ."

Throughout *The Ladies Man,* Herbert comments on his own re-actions and his own situation: "Ooh, I'm scared to death" (when the fearsome animal Baby is loose); his hand burning on the toaster (in an ineffable moment of delayed sensation); his button caught in Mrs. Wellenmelon's flower (the TV show); the skin of his back caught in the crack of the door that someone has closed on him (the mail-delivery sequence). These commentaries make the event present while distancing and banishing it, situating it in the reality of bodies and in the quasi-reality of things reported, and presenting the body, too, as wavering between those two spheres, proposing processes of thought, feeling, and sensation as purely optional aspects of experience and identity (speeches like the one in *The Patsy* have a rapidly self-correcting, self-denying quality, as if the Lewis character were rewriting his own being and commenting on the process of doing so).

At the lair of the nefarious Fong (Leonard Stone) in *The Big Mouth*, Clamson not only describes to the crooks what is happening to him but explains the patterns of his behavior: "If I detect hostility in people, I tend to submerge my inner emotional structure. Now, to expound on what I feel in my heart. . . ." Lewis can rarely resist giving the expression of self-insight a parodic form (the speech is heard in voiceover on a shot of the unsympathetic Bambi [Jeannine Riley] in the doorway, which further distances Clamson from us), just as in *Which Way to the Front?*, Byers expresses his self-insight in the language of late-sixties/early-seventies U.S. pop psychology (one of the many anachronisms with which this film, set in 1943, is sprinkled): "I can't say yes to no. I have to say no to no."

These Lewisian self-commentaries are invariably addressed to an interlocutor, who is usually silent (as in the scene in *The Patsy*), or to the camera. They are not closed circuits; they acknowledge and depend on the presence of the viewer as a potential supporter: the self-commentary goes toward the reverse field and seems hopeful of getting back from it a look, and laughter, that would make the happening more present and more distanced. Yet the absence of the owner of the look and the real absence of the interlocutor are strongly marked. The Lewis character is the one who feels and metamorphoses; the interlocutor might well be made of stone (as Maximilian's face seems to be in *Cinderfella*). Again, this structure dates back to Martin and Lewis. In Lewis's words, "'These were two guys who were in love with each other. They adored one another. One that could show it, and one that couldn't'" (qtd. in Bukatman 199). Lewis had the filmmaking insight, when he ascended to directing, to translate Martin's absence into a purely cinematic figure to play against: the reverse field, a site of desolation and rejection from which nothing comes back, completing the Lewis character's solitude.

The line between field and reverse field is a break. Instead of fusion there is a confrontation between the two fields. In cinema, the extreme, pure form of confrontation—the 180–degree cut—has something absolute about it. It can be felt as a violation (of "the 180–degree rule"), or it can be felt as the revelation that space is occupied, that what is absent from one field is present in another, that every shot is taken from a point in space that necessarily excludes itself from its optical field. Jean-Pierre Oudart writes: "Within the framework of a cinematic *énoncé* constructed on a shot/reverse-shot principle, the appearance of a lack perceived as a Some One (the Absent One) is followed by its abolition by someone (or something) placed within the same field" (46–47). Contrary to Oudart's claim that cinema (in the process he calls "suture," borrowing a term from Lacanian psychoanalytic theory) always abolishes or fills its lacks (thus promoting the illusion of the presence of the subject in "the signifying chain" of discourse), Lewis's cinema confronts the shot and its reverse shot with each other in a meeting that fails to reduce a fundamental incompatibility between them. The two shots encounter each other not as a lack and its fulfillment, a question and its answer, or a cause and its effect, but rather as two parallel surfaces.

A striking example of such a confrontation occurs in *The Errand Boy.* On the first day on his new job, Morty is introduced to Mr. Wabenlottnee (Benny Rubin) of the wardrobe department. The man tries to simplify the introduction for Morty by dictating his own name syllable by syllable. The cutting volleys between two frontal close-ups, one of Wabenlottnee, the other of Morty (each of whom looks directly into the camera—the effect is extraordinary, as if speech had become directly visible): the man speaks a syllable, then Morty repeats it, and so forth. But, at the end of the series, when Morty tries to put the whole name together, it comes out something like "Babonottin."

Another example occurs in *The Patsy,* during Stanley's unsuccessful rehearsal for his debut at the Copa Café. His stumbling monologue is broken up after each phrase by a cut to a reverse shot of Chic moaning as if in pain. Earlier in the film, Stanley wanders around the parlor of Professor Mueller (Hans Conreid), trying out various antique chairs and upsetting, but catching, vases and other objects, while, in shots intercut with Stanley's antics, Mueller watches and reacts in silent anguish. In all these sequences, the duration of the intercutting becomes felt not only as a source of humor but also as an additional source of strangeness. The shot triggers its reverse shot; the reverse shot punctuates the shot. Nothing passes between one shot and the other. The course of one shot is not altered because of the other; they represent two independent processes confronting each other but not leading to any synthesis—if anything, they lead to an anti-suture, since not only the "subject" but also any form of imaginary coherence and any totalizing "signifying chain" are excluded and denied.

Although the onscreen character's look plays a role in the functioning of the reverse field, Lewis's cinema reveals that there is another onscreen element that more fundamentally constitutes the reverse field: the face. Lewis's cinema (like Cassavetes's) is to a great extent a cinema of faces: their expressiveness or concealedness; the face as a suffering, sensitive membrane faithfully expressing internal processes (as Stanley philosophizes in *The Patsy*, "I always say that the eyes are the windows of the soul, and if shades are up, then . . .") or as an impassive surface blocking and denying them.

Sometimes a person looking at the Lewis character looks straight at the camera, while he, in the complementary shot, does not. In the first long sequence of *The Patsy*, the dead Wally's immobilized handlers stand like statues in a wide medium shot, staring at the camera, transfixed by the apparition of Stanley with his ice. Later, a series of close-ups shows each of them looking directly at the camera ("Do we look dishonest?"); in the reverse close shot of Stanley, he looks slightly away from the camera lens. In *The Nutty Professor*, there is a "subjective" traveling shot ostensibly from Love's point of view as he approaches the Purple Pit, passing a succession of people who stare, frozen, at the camera. The Lewis character often has the ability to strike people dumb with awe or disbelief and freeze them. An extreme example is in *The Big Mouth*, in which the apparition of Clamson emerging from the water causes Gunner (Vern Rowe) to become paralyzed on all fours. Later in the film, first Studs (Buddy Lester) and then Rex (Charlie Callas) are reduced to gibbering by the sight of Clamson. In *The Nutty Professor*, Buddy Lester's bartender is turned into a statue not by the sight of Buddy Love but by a taste of the Alaskan Polar-Bear Heater he has just mixed under Love's direction.

Lewis writes: "Some film-makers believe that you should never have an actor look directly into the camera. They maintain it makes the audience uneasy, and interrupts the screen story. I think it is nonsense, and usually have my actors, in a single, look direct into the camera at least once in a film if a point is to be served" (*Total Film-Maker* 120–21). In *The Nutty Professor*, after Buddy suddenly leaps over a wall and vanishes during their first private meeting, Stella turns and stares at the camera. She does so again after Buddy's staggering exit out of the Purple Pit, where he has just abandoned his attempt to sing "I'm in the Mood for Love." In *The Ladies Man,* Herbert turns to the camera to repeat one word from the stream of rapturous and admiring phrases a Marilyn Monroe–like starlet has just addressed to him: "Blond?" At the curtain calls that conclude *The Nutty Professor* and *The Patsy,* each of the main actors walks toward and looks into the camera.

The look toward the camera reaches out of the space of the film to confront the viewer. In *The Big Mouth,* in which the tendency reaches its height, this is accomplished inaugurally—by the narrator—then repetitively and systematically throughout the film. During the tennis-lesson scene, Bambi looks at the camera blankly, as if amazed by Clamson's ineptitude (like the nurse in Tashlin's *The Disorderly Orderly* who stares at the camera, stunned, while Jerome entraps her and himself in the bandage he is wrapping around a patient). Later, Clamson looks at the camera to repeat, uncomprehendingly, Suzie's parting words: "A cold shower?" When he realizes that Webster, the FBI man, is delusional, Clamson stares at the camera in shock. Suzie, alone in the kitchen after Clamson yells "I love you!" in her ear (before leaving to rejoin the gangster in the living room), turns to look at the camera. Studs looks at the camera while Gunner, who apparently imagines himself to be a dog, relieves himself by a tree at Sea World.

Clamson's stare at the camera in the scene with the delusional Webster implies the dawning of shared knowledge. It is also an extreme form of a kind of look toward the camera that has a long history in film comedy, and whose locus classicus is the work of Laurel and Hardy. This look implies or assumes complicity and like-thinking, and it expresses the helplessness and aloneness of the onscreen person who, driven to frustration, has no one to turn to except us. The look toward the camera is an appeal for help and sympathy, as if the viewer were, potentially, the double of the onscreen character, or as if the character were the viewer's onscreen delegate who endures, reacts, suffers, and struggles on the viewer's behalf and in the viewer's absence. But Clamson's look is extreme because the look, the scene, and their context together make it clear that no help is sought or expected: it is just a formal gesture, a signifier of the request for help, produced in a hopeless situation. The direct gaze at the camera becomes the sign of failed communication: a request for sympathy or help, or an appeal for unity that mistakes its mark and merely asserts the apartness of the appealing character.

Sometimes the internal properties of the image designate a look in a Lewis film as a subjective shot. In *The Ladies Man*, Herbert puts on his glasses, and in the reverse shot, the girls in the cafeteria come into focus. Earlier in the film, the camera executes a succession of jerky zoom-ins on a Help Wanted sign as seen from Herbert's point of view as he waits at the bus stop across the street. In both shots, vision is defective: if Herbert, or another Lewis character, is a "misfit" (as Warren Nefron in *Cracking Up* calls himself), it's not only because of his external characteristics but because of the way he sees the world. *The Nutty Professor* contains a series of "internally subjective" shots: the ninety-degree canted shot of Stella from the point of view of Kelp, horizontal on the shelf; the out-of-focus subjective shot from the point of view of Kelp, who has removed his glasses, of people in the bowling alley lined up like bowling pins; the traveling shot from Love's point of view as he makes his way to the Purple Pit; the shot of Stella listening to Love serenade her on piano, as smoke from his cigarette wafts into the shot from behind the camera; Stella slowly coming into focus when Kelp, during his confession speech, puts his glasses on. In one extraordinary shot, points of view diverge, and narrative purposes fall out of alignment: as Stella talks to Kelp about how innocuous the notorious Purple Pit is, the camera tracks in to a close-up of her; when the camera frames her in the close-up, the image becomes diffused. At the end of the shot, she looks at the camera and blinks.

In *The Family Jewels*, Donna looks into the lens of Uncle Julius's camera, which becomes, momentarily, *our* lens (in an iris shot). Later, Julius adjusts the mount in front of his camera (which is *our* camera), the mount becoming visible as a frame within the frame and emphasizing the composed nature of the image and the arbitrariness inherent in composition. This moment recalls Lewis's curtain call (in character as Kelp) in *The Nutty Professor*, during which he stumbles and falls into the camera lens. In the scene of the three crooks visiting Gunner in the hospital in *The Big Mouth*, there is a low-angle subjective shot of Thor caressing the camera lens.

In Lewis, the lens is not merely a point in space, an abstract function that organizes images, or a metaphor for consciousness grasping the world. The lens is a physical thing. Lewis relates point of view to the material existence of the camera and the physical position it occupies in space. In *The Family Jewels,* Julius repeatedly presses his finger onto the lens of his camera to show Donna where to look; he even comments on this gesture, "You'll have a face full of fingers." In *The Bellboy,* Stanley, carrying cigarettes, newspapers, and other items into a room filled with négligée-wearing female models, advances to the foreground and prudishly covers the lens with the palm of his hand. In the ball sequence in *One More Time,* Charlie's long-suppressed sneeze finally erupts as he lurches forward, Kelp-like, into the camera lens. The cut shows a reverse field in which already—in the instant of the cut—the exaggerated force of the sneeze has toppled a group of party guests, who slowly start picking themselves up from the floor (like the animated suits of armor in *The Errand Boy*).

Characters move toward the foreground to block the lens (in *The Errand Boy,* a prop man who picks up the "dummy" Morty to find it coming alive in his arms runs into the camera in terror) or withdraw from the lens to reveal the scene (as when Mr. Sneak enters Mr. Paramutual's office). In the *Sullivan Show* skit in *The Patsy,* Stanley, after his elaborate costume transformation, walks into the camera; Lewis then cuts to Stanley walking away from the camera, down the red carpet, and into the theater. At the end of *The Family Jewels,* Donna and Willard walk into the camera; there is a cut, and then they are walking away from the camera. In the disco fantasy sequence of *Hardly Working,* Bo pulls his dancing partner (SanDee Pitnick) into a 180–degree reverse shot across the cut. This sort of cut is not, of course, Lewis's invention, but it takes on a heightened value in his work because of the importance of a range of figures linked to the reverse field and the physical place of the camera in his films.

The most extreme reversal in Lewis's work is the ending of *The Patsy,* in which the reverse field of every film shot—the field containing the camera and the crew—is finally revealed. The tossed-off quality of the ending (parrying Ina Balin's calling him "a complete nut," Lewis remembers that he's having "nuts and whipped cream for lunch" and leads the cast and crew off the set, as his remarks trail off rather than reaching a neat period) perhaps acknowledges the impossibility of ending: the subject of this implicitly autobiographical film being still alive, the film cannot close (as Lewis says, "The people in the theater know I ain't gonna die; . . . I'm gonna make more movies, so I couldn't die"—the latter is also a statement of the endlessness of art). This ultimate reverse field of *The Patsy* is a place of seeming nonexistence and unimportance; even in being shown it appears less real than the space that its showing reveals to have been fictional. Nothing matters here (the stakes of the narrative having already been twice denied, first in Ellen's refusal of the wife role in Stanley's proposed romantic couple, second in Stanley's putative death by falling), so Lewis erases the space in the act of showing it: a way of remaining discreet about his own activity as director.

Oedipus Is No Problem

The "it's-a-movie" ending of *The Patsy* gives a specific and extreme form to an ambiguity that persists throughout Lewis's cinema. One of the most revolutionary aspects of *The Bellboy* is its reintroduction of the fantastic within a representational context defined (within and outside the film, by its genre) as naturalistic. The periodic appearances of the Stan Laurel surrogate played by Bill Richmond, the inexplicable powers that enable Stanley to fulfill impossible tasks like setting up hundreds of chairs in a hall or landing an airplane, and the fantasy conducting sequence are all instances in which the naturalistic—indeed, documentary-like—surface of the film is suddenly disturbed. Lewis's predilection for the fantastic survives in his later work: for example, in the Miss Cartilage sequence in *The Ladies Man,* the scenes with the clown hand-puppet and Magnolia in *The Errand Boy,* and the freezing of Thor's men into animal postures in *The Big Mouth.* These incursions of the fantastic point to a basic ambiguity in Lewis's films: the difficulty of determining what mode of representation is in force at a given moment. It is often difficult to determine the context in which a scene should be understood.

This uncertainty regarding context is related to another kind of ambiguity that can make watching Lewis's films uncomfortable. His work is full of scenes of direct or near-direct addresses to the audience, of confessions (*The Nutty Professor, Three on a Couch*); scenes of crisis in which characters find themselves alone, deprived of external recognition or support, and summon the strength to come to terms with their own natures and abilities and carry on (*The Patsy, One More Time, Which Way to the Front?*); scenes in which people affirm to each other the value of simple "goodness" or "niceness" (*The Ladies Man, The Big Mouth*). At the middle of the scathing depiction of show-business style and culture in *The Patsy,* Ellen speaks for feeling and for the heart: "We've been happy working as a family, and we hate the thought of breaking up." Ellen has the articulateness about feelings that is common to Lewis's heroines. Talking with Stanley backstage at the TV studio, she evokes "the tender, nice things, the things we wish would still prevail, but since they don't, we try to bring them back by remembering." She concludes: "The sweet things and the good things aren't always the things that make us better people. . . . If we can carry on after a bad thing happens, then we've grown up some." Suzie in *The Big Mouth* speaks with the same purified vocabulary: "You're good, you're nice."

The forthrightness of such talk may make Lewis's films appear mawkish, easily readable, and bathetic. Yet the films harbor a deep uncertainty that always stands ready to undermine what seem to be their own most firmly held values and basic imperatives, even as Lewis's insistence on sentiment threatens to become a parody of obviousness. Lewis's parodic impulse takes the form of a sententiousness that not only has no fear of parodying itself but doesn't even worry whether the parody is understood as parody: ambiguity is ever-present in Lewis, at least as a threat.

Consider the paradoxical romanticism of the beautifully lit high-angle close shot (highlights glittering in the pupils) of the studio singer (Rita Hayes) who overdubs "Lover" in *The Errand Boy.* For a magical moment, the scene opposes her belief in the song to the falseness of the scene on the screen. It is not clear what reaction Lewis wants this image to elicit, just as in *The Nutty Professor,* it is hard to tell how we are meant to react to the diffusing filter that transforms the close-up of Stella. Does Lewis offer the distortion of Kelp's vision as an object for laughter, or is he claiming this way of seeing Stella as his own and, as author of the film, challenging us to accept or reject his vision? The uncertainty is radical and uncomfortable. For every impulse toward affirmation, Lewis demonstrates an equally strong impulse toward negation. The "Lover" dubbing sequence in *The Errand Boy* confirms this when, after the professional singer finishes her successful take, the redubbed scene, during a public preview, turns out to have been *re*-redubbed, as Morty's offkey screeching issues from the onscreen actress's mouth.

In the scene of Elizabeth and Chris dancing to a slow ballad in *Three on a Couch*, the composition, the camera movement, the singer's direct address to the couple, and above all Janet Leigh's performance characterize this dance as an idyllic moment of understanding and togetherness. Throughout the long take, Chris's back is to the camera, which stays on Elizabeth's face. When the dance is over and Elizabeth returns to the table, Chris remains on the dance floor: though standing, he is asleep, and we realize that he may have been asleep throughout the dance without Elizabeth's knowledge. The final joke retroactively throws into question the romanticism of the scene without invalidating it—Lewisian ambiguity remains in force at all levels.

Lewis ridicules or ignores much of what is often sentimentalized: starting with the family and the family home, which become targets of satirical attack in all his films, and moving on to the paternalisms of capital and nation (as in *Which Way to the Front?*). When, in *The Ladies Man,* Mrs. Wellenmelon attempts to manipulate Herbert into staying on as her houseboy by pretending to weep, or when Herbert tells Katie of his traumatic graduation day (a story that reduces her to tears) and of the death of Marvin the goldfish (an event in which Herbert's continued emotional investment puzzles even Katie), Lewis's critique of sentimentality could not be clearer.

Yet, in the same film, Lewis provides a naturalistic, muted treatment of the relationship (which never becomes a love story) between the isolated Fay and the compassionate Herbert. At one point, there is a beautiful fadeout on a medium close shot of Fay practicing dancing: she continues her dance after Walter Scharf's score has reached a sting and as the final note dies. The delicacy of this moment is of a kind that Lewis knows how to bring out through the fadeout. We find it again in *The Family Jewels* in the scene that fades out on Willard listening alone to the record of "This Diamond Ring" (a then-recent pop hit by Lewis's son, Gary Lewis), and in *The Errand Boy* at the end of Morty's encounter with Magnolia. Such moments introduce into their films something that functions less as sentimentality than as a naturalistic (and noncomedic) softening of the harshness of the surrounding comedy.

In *The Errand Boy,* Morty tells Magnolia of his desire, while he was in his native New Jersey, to go to Hollywood to be closer to the movies: "I guess it wasn't uncommon with me like with a lot of other guys my age that liked movies. . . . So when I got here I realized I wasn't any closer to it than when I was in New Jersey. And as you know, when you're far away from something you can't get to it. That's not quite half as bad as when you're close to that something and you can't get to it. Right?" Here, Lewisian sentimentality is explicitly pathos—that is, distance. Morty's confession turns this satire of Hollywood in *The Errand Boy* inside out, making it into a statement of longing for an inner truth of Hollywood— probably the same inner truth that attracted Lewis himself when he was a movie lover, long before he became a moviemaker (see my interview with him in this book)—that becomes paradoxically less accessible the closer he gets to its origin. Andrew Sarris criticizes Lewis's sentimentality as sanctimonious on the grounds that Lewis is guilty of "playing the innocent" and of failing to acknowledge a contradiction between, on one side, his own sophistication and "professional knowingness" about show business and, on the other side, what Sarris calls "his simpering simple-mindedness on the screen" and the "conformist, sentimental, and banal" messages of his films (242–44). Far from failing to acknowledge this contradiction, however, *The Errand Boy* makes it as glaring as possible by allowing Morty to speak of his distance from his dream of cinema. *The Errand Boy* is neither a celebration nor an evisceration of Hollywood; it is a mourning of it, a lament for its disappearance.

If Lewis's films admittedly contain much of the kind of moralizing that Sarris objects to (as when, in *The Family Jewels*, Donna asserts that Willard should be her father, or when, near the end of *The Ladies Man*, Fay criticizes the other girls for trying to keep Herbert from leaving the house), they also contain the antidote to it, in such moments as the parodic moralizing of Leo Durocher in *The Errand Boy* ("Be kind and be sweet"). In *Cracking Up*, Warren, doing his job as parking valet, is entrusted by Sammy Davis Jr. with his car. After Davis goes off, having asked Warren to treat the car with care, Warren, alone in the frame, simpers, "What a wonderful human being." Those who have heard Lewis, as host of the Muscular Dystrophy Association telethon or on a TV talk show, speak of Davis (his close friend) in similar terms may perceive this line as a conscious self-parody and an invitation to share in a point of view from which such encomiums, delivered by one show-business figure about another, appear glib and empty. Is Lewis disavowing the sentiment? Criticizing Davis? Or himself? What, if anything, is being suggested about the "character" of Warren here? When Lewis faces the camera to praise Davis, does Warren even exist as a character? Lewis's films constantly put in question their own implied underlying meanings. Because the context he sets up is basically a show-business context—in which persons and their meanings are always constantly performed—the possibility always exists for a second- (or a third-, or a fourth-) degree reading of meanings as simulated or disavowed.

There are few unconditionals in Lewis's sentimentality. Children should be loved and protected (*The Family Jewels, Hardly Working*), but they can also be labeled "monsters" by the Lewis character himself (*The Errand Boy*), with whom they may have a hostile, adversarial relationship (as does the young son of Bo's girlfriend, Millie [Deanna Lund], in *Hardly Working*). Sentimentality has to do with protecting things as they are, with not growing up and growing old, with permanent childhood—a condition of which Lewis is undoubtedly the greatest poet in American cinema. This is why "In Dreams They Run" (1970), Lewis's episode for the TV series *The Bold Ones,* is so startling: it faces the death of a child (in the image of an empty bed) with blunt directness. *Three on a Couch* is a parable, a kind of bachelor-party farewell to childhood. The figure of the male psychiatric patient sucking on a pacifier in the opening-titles sequence (an action that Lewis repeats in *Which Way to the Front?*) externalizes the limitations of childishness.

"A Little Fun to Match the Sorrow" (1965), Lewis's episode for the hospital TV series *Ben Casey,* opposes the compulsive joking of a neurosurgeon-in-training, Green (Lewis), to the grimness of the resident surgeon, Casey (Vincent Edwards). Green pretends that he is merely trying to insert some humanity and humor into the work; to Casey, lightheartedness is dangerous. There is no obvious way to reconcile the two positions, and Lewis, as director, embraces neither. Except with Buddy Love in *The Nutty Professor* and Uncle Everett in *The Family Jewels,* Lewis has never gone so far in criticizing his own characters as in "A Little Fun to Match the Sorrow"—a criticism that is all the more striking in that Green is close in many ways to Lewis's typical lovable Idiot characters (and not atypical like Buddy and Everett). In a disturbing scene, Green, unable to tell his estranged girlfriend (Dianne Foster) that her sick father's prognosis is poor, tries to dodge her questions and seems about to break into typical Lewisian double talk, only to receive the woman's sharp rebuke. If Lewis's work can be called a flight from reality, from adulthood, and from death into comedy, "A Little Fun to Match the Sorrow" constitutes the most brutal and self-contradicting arrest of this flight.

The Big Mouth, a film of protest, is (with *Which Way to the Front?*) perhaps the least sentimental of Lewis's films. *The Big Mouth* continues the movement away from childhood and into adulthood that Lewis started in *Three on a Couch.* Like Chris Pride, Gerald Clamson does not have childhood, or childlikeness, for an alibi. He is a solitary, isolated figure, with no family and no past, defined only by his profession and his hobby. More than any other Lewis character, he is a person with no qualities and no strengths (and also no weaknesses)—in short, no character to draw on. And Lewis asks for him none of the fond indulgence he seems to expect the viewer to bestow on his characters in *The Errand Boy* or *The Patsy* (unlike them, Clamson is not inept or accident-prone). Some of the same things can be said of Byers in *Which Way to the Front?*; his great wealth makes him an even less obvious recipient of automatic sympathy than Clamson.

Clamson's normality and undistinguishedness put the emphasis of the film elsewhere than on the feelings of humiliation or inadequacy that haunt the Lewis characters in *The Ladies Man, The Nutty Professor, Which Way to the Front?, Hardly Working,* and *Cracking Up.* With a certain austerity, *The Big Mouth* sets out to define what remains of the human in a mechanized, programmed world. In scene after scene, *The Big Mouth* exposes a society devoted to annihilation: Thor strafing, then torpedoing the beach, leaving a huge hole (from the bottom of which Valentine's voice resonates); the hotel manager and his men enumerating the various ways they will kill Clamson; the gangsters aiming their guns at Clamson from various directions; Fong gloating over his horrific bubbling vat. The film takes all this violence somewhat seriously—that is, not purely as a subject for entertainment. It stages moments that clash violently with the expected style and themes of an innocuous comedy: unexpectedly, Fong has one of his men killed in a horrible manner (though offscreen); we might also be surprised by the "real" blood leaking from Valentine's skindiver suit (but as Godard said, "Not blood, red").

The Big Mouth is made up entirely of flight, of escape. Several great figures that proclaim a triumph over gravity organize the space of the film: first, the long-take helicopter shot at the beginning of the film that takes off, describes a short curve, then redescends; later, the movements of Clamson upward, onto roofs and into the air (escaping from the hotel manager, bouncing off the tennis-court net, fleeing from his adversaries). In the final sequence at Sea World, a veritable poem on escape, Clamson tries to hide in plain sight by assuming the disguise of a kabuki performer (trying to white himself out with the white face makeup); then, fallen into the crooks' clutches, he tries vainly to escape by making himself small, low, and imperceptible (after the fashion of Kelp's father in the flashback scene in *The Nutty Professor*); finally, he suddenly simply disappears from Fong's laboratory. In a sense, Clamson is continuing the movement of his normal life, which is itself an escape into the nonentity of the functionary, the quiet man, a zero degree of humanity (the same route that Bo attempts to take, without success, in *Hardly Working*). *The Big Mouth* defines the human being as a target, someone being chased: movement, escape, becoming imperceptible. (Compare, in the party sequence of *Three on a Couch,* Chris's anguished attempts to avoid having any of the four women he is involved with see him with any other.) Clamson is also a figure who goes too far and gives society more than it demands of him (just as Stanley in *The Bellboy* does). In doing so, he exposes the absurdity of its demands and rebels through an excess of conformity. (This is the principle of, for example, Kelp's agreeing with Warfield in *The Nutty Professor* when the latter declares their conversation to be finished.)

The outward conditions of the plot of each of Lewis's films are only mechanisms to let his character assume various disguises and to confront him again with the objects that have precipitated his flight. The hero rarely overcomes these objects directly; his triumph consists instead (as in *The Ladies Man*) in a trying-out, in the mode of play and fantasy, of various possible attitudes toward them. Still, in *The Big Mouth,* the anguish felt by the protagonist, or rather the success of the film at conveying his anguish, is heightened rather than diminished by his showing something like coolness in his attempts to bring his relations with the crooks onto a more normal social plane. This is in sharp contrast to such comedies as the Crosby and Hope films, in which Hope's wisecracks and departures from the frame of the fictional narrative imply his character's mastery of the narrative situation and the absence of real danger. In *The Big Mouth,* the danger remains real—though, of course, fictional.

Such generic discontinuity is a constant feature of Lewis's work. The long transformation sequence in *The Nutty Professor* is handled as it might be in an odd, but straight, horror movie. In *Which Way to the Front?,* the flashback of Hackle (Jan Murray) backstage at a nightclub, menaced by thugs, is played straight and could be from a serious, dark film on the sordid life of an unsuccessful nightclub comedian. In general, the first half of *Which Way to the Front?* is not very funny; it is not until the second half, with Byers's encounters with the German language and the Nazi enemy, that Lewis strikes comic gold. Fairly long stretches of *The Family Jewels* and *Hardly Working* and, perhaps, nearly all of *One More Time* are also lacking in humor. One of my premises is that Lewis's work creates an impure, shifting context within which such a lack need not be accounted a flaw. Changes in tone occur constantly in Lewis's comedies. In the long flashback of the high-school dance in *The Patsy,* he refuses to mitigate the pain of Stanley's humiliation. In *The Family Jewels,* the sour clown Uncle Everett and Donna's depressed reaction to him are played on a naturalistic level. In *The Errand Boy,* Morty's encounter with Magnolia steers the film away from slapstick and toward a low-key existential meditation, with overtones of the possible beginning of a romantic relationship.

Generic discontinuity pervades the history of American film comedy. Chaplin's films—from such spoofs as *Burlesque on Carmen* (1916) through the growing importance of pathos and emotion in his mature work—provide the model that was most important to Lewis. Such Martin and Lewis films as Taurog's *The Stooge* (1952) mix comedy with sentiment and seriousness; in *Dean and Me,* Lewis writes of his realization that artistic maturity depends upon this combination—a realization that he dates to the 1954 production of Joseph Pevney's *Three-Ring Circus* (significantly, the film that marked the first serious rift between Lewis and Martin), although he surely had inklings of it when he was making *That's My Boy* in 1951: "The one thing that Charlie [Chaplin] had—in spades—was something I'd barely tapped into: pathos. Great comedy, in my mind, always goes hand in hand with great sadness: This is the grand Circle of Life, the mixture of laughter and tears. You can be funny without tapping into strong emotion, but the humor is more superficial. Funny without pathos is a pie in the face. And a pie in the face is funny, but I wanted more" (Lewis and Kaplan 211).

Lewis's incorporation of pathos often involves structuring a film around a therapeutic theme: a character needs to be cured of some affliction or has a problem—at least partly internal—that needs to be solved. The therapeutic theme is prevalent throughout Lewis's films, including several he did not direct, such as *That's My Boy, The Delicate Delinquent, Cinderfella,* and *The Disorderly Orderly.* Although the therapeutic structure vanishes completely from *The Bellboy* (which treats neither Stanley's incompetence nor his muteness as issues for therapy) and becomes submerged in *The Ladies Man* (in which Herbert's problem—his fear of women—is never "solved"), it resurfaces in *The Nutty Professor.* Starting with its central premise—Kelp's transformation into Love—*The Nutty Professor* is concerned with forms of self-therapy. The therapeutic role Love plays for Kelp is also emphasized in Love's dealings with others. Encouraging Warfield to declaim Hamlet's "To be or not to be" soliloquy while standing on the table in his office, Buddy tells him: "You know it's the best thing in the world for you." Earlier, he kisses Stella and says, "That's good for you." The message Love brings to all (and it is echoed again in the intrusion of Kelp's father into Kelp's classroom at the end) is one of healing.

Though Lewis clearly feels (and expects the audience to feel) more affection for Kelp, it is obvious that Buddy Love is loved, too: the close-up of Stella looking at him as he sings "That Old Black Magic" is eloquent, as is the enthusiasm with which the crowd responds to his performance. Later, in the parked car, Buddy tells Stella, "You know darn well that nothing delights us more than being enjoyed, appreciated, or just plain liked by someone, right?" (see fig. 7). The addiction to this delight and the pain that accompanies its withdrawal account for Buddy's maudlin negativity on his second appearance, drunk, in the Purple Pit: "I think I'll do a tune that I'm going to record for Poverty Records. They're the only ones that'll have me" (Poverty Records is the name of the company for which Stanley Belt records his hit single in *The Patsy*).

In *Three on a Couch,* Lewis and Janet Leigh suggest that Elizabeth's devotion to her patients may be motivated as much by her own attachment to the role she plays in their lives as by her interest in helping

Figure 7. Stella Stevens and Jerry Lewis
in *The Nutty Professor.*

them. Robert Benayoun, in noting that the Elizabeth's problem exemplifies for Lewis "the key idea of professionally making people happy" (142), points out the central metaphor of the film. On the surface, the screenplay of *Three on a Couch* seems loaded against Elizabeth (indeed, against women) in defining the three patients' problem as an aversion to men and proposing the end of this aversion as marking their cure. To see the film from this point of view is to share Ben and Chris's implicit attitude that the three patients' problems are not deeply serious and that Elizabeth's concern for the women is misplaced and excessive. Seen more deeply, *Three on a Couch* becomes a film about the need for love and a restatement, in different terms and on a different plane, of the theme of *The Nutty Professor.* The problems of the three women are, for Lewis, serious (serious within the world of comedy and capable of resolution in comic terms), and he presents them as such. Through the mounting strain on Chris as he tries to carry out his plot and through the unraveling of the plot when the four women in his life come together, *Three on a Couch* demonstrates, contrary to its ostensible message, the absurdity of the (culturally encouraged) presumption that a man could be the solution to the problems of all women, emphasizing (like *The Nutty Professor*) the anxiety that results for someone who tries to act on the basis of that presumption.

A critique of the therapeutic/normative role of male sexuality, *Three on a Couch* is also a comment on its time and its society. Chris's constant smoking and drinking (and Ringo's unlit cigar), which outdo Buddy Love's indulgence in these habits in *The Nutty Professor,* suggest a parody of and a rebellion against the "adult" image Lewis felt compelled to adapt at this stage of his career. The implied derision of psychiatry is a sixties notation, as is the implicit sexism of Ben's plan (which is echoed by the tumbling of copies of *Playboy* from a diplomat's briefcase onto the street). Shortly before *Three on a Couch,* Lewis had played a subordinate part in another farce with which its plot shares a number of similarities, *Boeing Boeing,* starring Tony Curtis as an American reporter in Paris who conducts affairs with three different flight attendants while trying to keep them from meeting or finding out about each other. Quintessential Sixtiesiana, *Boeing Boeing* would fit comfortably among the films that Geoffrey O'Brien cites in *Dream Time* as paralleling the post–JFK assassination national mood shift to "hysterical lightheadedness": *The Pink Panther, A Shot in the Dark, Kiss Me Stupid, The Patsy* (sitting rather oddly among this company), *The World of Henry Orient, What's New Pussycat?, Lord Love a Duck, The Swinger, Don't Make Waves,* and Tashlin's *Caprice.* According to O'Brien, these films "aimed at frothy exuberance but were closer to the half-giddy, half-sickened disjointedness of a bunch of compulsive partygoers beginning to run out of steam." O'Brien accurately recognizes in this cycle a reflection of sixties modernity, "jagged and permanently out of kilter," obsessively dedicated to the pursuit of fun and the "religion of the fleeting instant," characterized by "an edgy failure to sustain any emotional note for long" (30). If *Three on a Couch* is Lewis's approximation of the mid-sixties sex comedy, it is also his critique and overcoming of it, his correction of *Boeing Boeing.* Chris refrains from exploiting his three conquests sexually ("Please tell her [Elizabeth] I was always a gentleman," he begs them at the end). Chris, too, remains a Lewisian innocent—a more mature one for whom sexuality is no longer innocent and who thus must make a conscious choice to maintain his innocence.

Discomfort with sexuality—and femininity—is visible in much of Lewis's work (as Benayoun and other French critics pointed out to him, to his professed bewilderment). Lewis regularly confronts feminine attractiveness with its reverse, as in *The Bellboy* when, after having slimmed down while staying at the hotel, Miss Hartung bloats up again to her previous enormous weight from eating the candy that Stanley gives her as a going-away present. Of the women in *The Errand Boy,* the closest to a fully realized and sympathetic character and an acceptable erotic object is Magnolia, the puppet; the glamorous and sexually available Serina (Felicia Atkins), the movie star who attaches Morty to herself at the Hollywood premiere, is rejected as an automaton, a not fully conscious being. Serina is another incarnation of one of Lewis's most hallucinatory creations, the model in *The Bellboy* who, moving in her sleep with an involuntary unbridledness, attaches herself to Stanley while sprawling on a couch in the hotel lobby. The eroticism of this image is inseparable from the woman's dependence and unconsciousness—traits that also characterize the three patients in *Three on a Couch.* Nevertheless, *Three on a Couch* enables Lewis to achieve a certain balance in his view of women. The film inverts the premise of *The Ladies Man:* instead of a man fleeing from women, Lewis shows three women fleeing from men. What remains constant is the figure of the man being embodied by a single actor, Lewis (albeit a Lewis who, characteristically, divides himself into several personalities), whereas the female figure is multiplied, whether she is conceived as the object or the subject of the obsession.

Lewis's cinema rejects the privileged structures of psychoanalysis: the Oedipus complex and the patriarchal family. If mother figures are invariably negative in Lewis's films (for example, Lewis in drag as Herbert's mother in *The Ladies Man*—a figure so repellent that Herbert turns her photo away from the camera; see also the terrifying, overpowerful mothers in *The Nutty Professor* and *Which Way to the Front?*), father figures are viewed no more positively: they are usually too aggressive, like the mailroom manager (Stanley Adams) in *The Errand Boy* and Frank in *Hardly Working.* In *Which Way to the Front?,* Byers kills the father (Kesselring) by impersonating him and taking his place, as Warren will do at the end of *Cracking Up.* Rather than merely marking the renewal of a never ending cycle, these acts are escapes from the cycle. In "In Dreams They Run," young Davey escapes, too: he decides to leave his biological parents to join the larger family of muscular-dystrophy sufferers and health-care professionals at the hospital.

At the end of *The Nutty Professor,* after following his son in taking the formula and transforming himself, the father goes beyond the son, becoming worse than him in commercializing the formula and assuming a salesman's role (whereas Buddy Love at least entertained people with his singing). Similarly, at the end of *Cracking Up,* the psychiatrist becomes a minor version of Warren. These imitations of the son by the father represent decisive victories over Oedipus. At the end of *The Errand Boy,* passing along the lineup of his former studio superiors in his Cadillac convertible limousine, Morty repeats his name-learning exercise from earlier in the film, this time with Mr. Babewosentall; but now, at the end of the syllable-by-syllable enunciation, it is the bearer of the name himself who mangles the whole name, making himself the butt of the joke and turning himself into an idiot in the presence of the self-assured star Morty. A father who, imitating the son's linguistic troubles, fails to pronounce his own name: surely this is the most ignoble version of the father.

In *Which Way to the Front?,* the ease with which Byers substitutes himself for Kesselring (after dispatching several of the latter's subordinates), no less than the ease with which he carries off his impersonation despite seemingly having no competence in the German language (by a movie convention that Lewis characteristically flaunts, the German officers all speak English), suggests Lewis's derision of the Oedipal scenario. It is, after all, no big deal to insert oneself into language, to displace the father and assume his name.

"Home" does not exist in Lewis's world. His biography offers an explanation for this absence: his parents, vaudeville performers, were constantly on the road. In *The Family Jewels,* whose story can be described as a child's search for a home, Donna and Willard appear to live in hotels, and at the end of the film it is not clear where they will go. The boxlike spaces of Lewis's films are never spaces of domestic comfort but stages for performance. Karl Marx writes that the worker "is at home when he is not working, and when he is working he is not at home" (110). In Lewis's first three films, which are all about work, only in *The Ladies Man* do we briefly see where the Lewis character sleeps. (In later films, he provides more glimpses of his characters' intimate lives: the bed scene in *The Nutty Professor,* the hotel room scene in *The Family Jewels,* and a few scenes in Bo's bedroom in *Hardly Working.*) In *The Bellboy,* the bell captain tells his staff: "What you do after working hours is *our* business." If home is a space for the private individual, there is no home for the bellboys. Near the end of the film, the hotel manager

Novak, denouncing Stanley at a union meeting of the bellboys, says, "I've given you a home away from home, and this is the way you repay me." The home away from home is a palace—a parody of the idea of home as a place of comfort scaled to its occupants. In *The Errand Boy*, the back of his jacket collar impaled on a hook, Morty must spend the night upright among a group of mannequins (until in the morning a prop assistant mistakes him for a dummy and starts to carry him away).

If home is that from which one is exiled and to which one cannot return, the problem for the individual becomes that of learning to love this state of permanent flight and making it the condition for a greater universality. Lewis is always skeptical about, if not opposed to, a merely personal quest for self-knowledge (at the end of *The Nutty Professor*, Kelp is unaware that Stella has purchased two bottles of his father's "tonic": it is a secret she shares with the viewer while winking at the camera). Advised by the psychiatrist Karl Menninger that he should refrain from undergoing analysis, Lewis knew why without needing to be told: "'If I find out what's bothering me, I won't be funny any more'" (qtd. in Benayoun 143). Show business constitutes, for Lewis, an alternate psychoanalysis, a therapeutic sphere in which he acts out his obsessions in public and transcends them (see the confession scene at the prom in *The Nutty Professor*). In several films, Lewis depicts show business as an alternate family. Herbert's progress in *The Ladies Man* takes him from his real, triangular family to the surrogate family of Mrs. Wellenmelon's collection of would-be starlets. In *The Patsy*, Ellen calls the group formed by the handlers "a family." The forming of the private army in *Which Way to the Front?* resembles the forming of a theatrical troupe as much as it does the forming of a surrogate family.

The link between therapy and comedy is one of the mainsprings of Lewis's work, from at least as early as the partnership with Martin. Echoing sociological interpretations of Martin and Lewis's ascent in anxious postwar America, Lewis remarks: "What we really were, in an age of Freudian self-realization, was the explosion of the show-business id" (Lewis and Kaplan 7). One of Lewis's innovations is making the show-business id the instrument and the vehicle of a superior alternate model of self-realization to that of psychoanalysis. From the "magic potion" the Hollywood studios are said (at the beginning of *The Errand Boy*) to brew to Kelp's formula in *The Nutty Professor* is but a short step.

How to Undo Things with Words

A motif in Lewis is the magic word, password, or "order-word"[5] that starts the plot by summoning the characters to assume their places in it. The word "Who?", uttered by an exasperated Caryl Ferguson (Everett Sloane) in *The Patsy* as he ponders finding an unknown person and making him into a star, sets the plot in motion. Similarly, in *The Errand Boy,* Morty is chosen as "someone nobody knows." The will in *The Family Jewels,* the plan to "cure" the three women in *Three on a Couch,* and the dying gangster's exhortation in *The Big Mouth* are all examples of order-words that start the plots of the films (whereas the title word "Smorgasbord" magically *stops* the plot of a film better known under its video release title, *Cracking Up*). In *Which Way to the Front?,* the magic word, uttered by the recruiting officer (Myron Healey), is "rejection"—the same word that resonates, unspoken, behind the graduation-day sequence of *The Ladies Man,* in which the sight of his beloved in the arms of another man sends Herbert on his flight, and behind the laying-off of Bo at the beginning of *Hardly Working,* in which it is not an individual, a government, or a company but an entire economic and cultural system that issues the damning rejection of the circus employees and of the circus as a form of mainstream entertainment—a rejection that the film and its hero will turn around.

The whole of *The Bellboy* is a series of instructions, each one giving rise to a block of cinema that is not only the carrying out of the instruction but the depiction of a breakdown that results from its carrying out (told to take everything out of the trunk of a guest's Volkswagen Beetle, Stanley shows up at its owner's room bringing the motor), the realization of a possibility that the order (which is explicitly concerned only with the single "correct" outcome it envisions) contains and suppresses. The Lewisian block is a kind of deprogramming, a loosening of the potential for chaos in the order. It is a contradictory, paradoxical way of refusing the order (and also the order of orders, the regime of the order, this way of determining the potentials of language). Orders are never merely given and accepted; they have to be processed and understood—and in the process, subverted. In *The Errand Boy,* we hear Morty's garbled attempt to repeat Mr. Paramutual's instructions (take wife to medical building, get car washed) over a medium shot of Morty driving off in the car; by the time he reaches the car wash in the next scene, the two parts of the order have evidently become conflated, so that the wife is going to get washed with the car; and what was not explicit in the order—secure the top of the convertible before having it washed—is merely ignored. The literal repetition of an order is no guarantee that it has been understood: in *Which Way to the Front?*, Bland (Steve Franken), reduced to a robot or a moron, repeats his wife's commands verbatim—so that, as when children try to be annoying, personal pronouns get applied to the wrong person ("Make me a sandwich." "Make me a sandwich." "No, make *me* a sandwich." "No, make *me* a sandwich").

Failure characterizes the receiver's side of the communication act in Lewis's films. In *The Big Mouth,* Clamson and Suzie talk at cross purposes in his hotel suite. Misunderstanding his litany of phrases such as "frustrated," "can't stop thinking about it," "you're the first one this week" (who would listen to him), and "I can't get it off of my mind" (his "problem"), the offended Suzie retorts: "Why don't you try a cold shower?" The scene exists for no other reason than to demonstrate the failure of understanding, primordial in Lewis's universe.

Like Stanley in *The Bellboy,* Morty in *The Errand Boy* distinguishes himself by his propensity for subversion and disturbance, for liberating the fulfillment of an order from the issuing of an order. Morty's misadventures at the studio expose the mechanics of filmmaking as an impersonal process in which anonymous and interchangeable people labor to glorify unimpressive stars and antiquated stories. An entire production system, and an entire cultural system, function on automatic pilot. Lewis's criticism takes on not only filmmaking but the collective unconscious. Attending a premiere, the starlet Serina blithely mistakes Morty for her escort for the evening and carries on an extended one-sided conversation with him as if they had been intimates for years. In the script-typing room, Morty, by tripping over a garbage can, triggers a cataclysm of tumbling pages and shuffled genres (the viewer is left to imagine the film that would result if the script were collated and shot).

The mere act of issuing an order is so potent, so threatening, that the person to whom it is issued, if that person is played by Jerry Lewis, may rush off to complete it before hearing what the order is. Already familiar with this danger, the bell captain (Bob Clayton) in *The Bellboy* issues an instruction that expects to be misunderstood rather than followed: he points at a steamer trunk, and Stanley, following the line of his point, assumes he's being asked to fetch the trunk itself, which he does, with great effort, only to be told (by the man who has been standing frozen all the while, his pointing arm extended) that what was required was only the hat box that was on top of the trunk (see fig. 8). Similarly, in *The Ladies Man,* Gainsborough says, "I've come to see my girl," and Herbert, accompanied by a cartoon sound effect, dashes out of the frame, leaving Gainsborough waiting for Herbert to return to get the girl's name. The bell captain's is a false instruction, like Balling's instructions to Bo in *Hardly Working* (which Bo, after first claiming not to understand them, mouths along with Balling as the latter heavily repeats them, with additional details)—the true content of the command is its demonstration of the superiority of the commanding person. In another sense, the bell captain's command resembles Valentine's initial order to Clamson in *The Big Mouth.* As during each pause for breath his listener starts dashing off, Valentine gasps: "Hurry! Wait!" All goals are like this: we are sent after them in a hurry but also told to wait, not to go too fast: time is dual, both urgent and extended; contradiction is built into the demand at the beginning.

A pedantic language often characterizes the order. In *The Errand Boy,* the needlessly detailed way Morty's mailroom manager describes the things he is to carry—"packages, envelopes, papers, and other matter"—

Figure 8. The steamer trunk in *The Bellboy:*
Bob Clayton and Jerry Lewis.

makes it clear that there is a text behind the command and that the person has been reduced to being the loudspeaker of the text. Early in *The Patsy*, Ferguson says to Stanley: "We know all we need to know, and all you need to find out is what we tell you." The discourse of the experts and bosses is complete, unchangeable, self-contained, and timeless. "What you do during working hours," the bell captain tells his men in *The Bellboy*, "is our business. And what you do after working hours is *our* business." The stress on "our" in the second sentence, instead of highlighting a contrast in meaning between the two sentences, becomes a parodic sign of the ownership of language that makes all issuing of commands tautological and thereby undoes itself.

As Gilles Deleuze and Félix Guattari write, "The order bears always and already on orders, which is why the order is redundancy" (95). Lewis unfolds redundancy for its own sake, *as redundancy*—in *The Ladies Man*, Herbert's account to Katie of his fateful graduation-day discovery of his beloved's infidelity triggers a flashback repetition of the scene (which we have seen only ten minutes before). This repetition discloses nothing new but only confirms the obsessive nature of Herbert's relation to the scene (and, in a wider sense, the obsessional character that all narrative possesses for Lewis).

Language itself is redundancy in Lewis's work. Characters repeat themselves or repeat what they have just heard. In *The Errand Boy*, Mr. Sneak compulsively repeats the words of his boss, Mr. Paramutual. At some moments of *Which Way to the Front?*, the only function of Byers's three sidekicks is merely to parrot, each in his turn, Byers's words. Lewis's characters speak in ways that call the communicative and referential functions of language into question. Communication is endlessly discussed as a possibility, an event, or a limit, as in the classic exchange that concludes Kelp's visit to the office of Dr. Warfield early in *The Nutty Professor:*

> WARFIELD: I'm sure that we won't have to have another little talk like this again. Am I correct in assuming this?
> KELP: Oh, uh, without question, you're absolutely—uh, yes, we'll never have to correct our talk. Uh, we won't ever speak. Ah, that is, we'll never have to talk again. We just never will discuss talking. Uh, we shouldn't really converse about speaking.
> WARFIELD: Professor, our discussion has come to an end.

The concept/model "won't talk" inspires in Kelp a series of revisions, the inadequacy of which he recognizes as soon as he produces them. Kelp understands what is being discussed, the signified, to be talking itself, while Warfield's intended meaning (that since Kelp will obey his command and desist from chemistry experiments in class, it will be unnecessary for the two men to talk again *on this particular topic*) disappears behind Kelp's restatements. This is a way of parodying and undoing authoritarian meaning—the command implicit in Warfield's words and in the hierarchical situation that Warfield has set up to his benefit (including the cushioned chair in which his guest slowly sinks)—by paying attention to expression. It is also more radical and thorough than that. Kelp's parody (uttered with a seeming innocuousness that serves as a protective mask) reduces all language to a conversation about speaking. If the theme of every utterance is always enunciation itself, the order is undone in advance by the impossibility of executing it outside the circuit of language.

In *Hardly Working,* during Bo's interview in Frank's office, Frank asks, "Now you say you never worked for the post office before?" Bo, his mouth filled with the doughnut he has been eating, replies with an extended passage of gibberish. This way of answering the question ridicules the idea that it can be or needs to be answered and furthermore casts into doubt whether a question has even been asked, whether information could be exchanged or new information produced within the ceremonial context of this interview.

There is a class of characters in Lewis's films who have been given the voice and who are supposed to speak on behalf of the system or the society and utter its truths: voices of authority. Examples include the New York director in *The Errand Boy,* who pronounces authoritatively on the unique brilliance of Morty's improvisation with a gargantuan erupting champagne bottle; the supposed FBI man in *The Big Mouth;* the recruiting officer in *Which Way to the Front?;* and the psychiatrist in *Cracking Up.* Again and again a voice makes itself heard that comes as if from the place of truth, where people are accepted or rejected, declared okay or not okay.

To counter this authoritarianism of language, Lewis uses languagelessness and other kinds of antilanguage. In *The Bellboy,* Stanley is silent "because no one ever asked" him to talk. (Compensating for his character's silence, the entirety of Lewis's film is an extremely sophisticated utterance by its author; in Lewis's directorial debut, filmmaking becomes both a substitute for and the privileged metaphor for speech.) Lewis revives the premise that no one cares what his character has to say for *The Big Mouth*; the pretext for the chain of zany happenings that befall Gerald Clamson and those with whom he comes into contact is that, as the onscreen narrator of the film says, "Most people are so completely wrapped up in their own affairs that they aren't really terribly interested in anything that doesn't involve them." (The "moral" discerned by the offscreen narrator at the end of *The Bellboy*: "You'll never know the next guy's story unless you ask.") People are blocks that come into contact with other blocks without becoming interested in or learning anything about each other. The Lewis character, in numerous films, is the casualty of this noninterest and the one for whom forming an attachment is still possible.

Lewis also undoes the tyranny of language through torrents of double talk. Noninformation proliferates in his films. Rutherford, in *Three on a Couch*, produces a lengthy, pseudoscientific discourse on Coleoptera—a chain of unfinished sentences that parodies learned discourse (like the TV-repair monologue in Tashlin's *It's Only Money*). Lewis's films abound in improvised-sounding verbal routines, such as Uncle Bugsy's stumbling monologues in *The Family Jewels:* "Nobody finds where I hide out. When I . . . when I . . . they ain't gonna . . . 'cause I really . . . hide. You have to really look to find me." In *Which Way to the Front?*, Byers, in his disguise, flummoxes a German checkpoint guard with German-accented double talk. At such moments, language is halfway between sound poetry and an absurdist and violent rejection of the possibility of communication. The checkpoint guard requests the password from the fake field marshal; Byers merely gets the guard to write the password down, then gives him his same password back. Instead of a passage from one to the other, a mirror movement has taken place.

Speechlessness, silence, or the other silence that is babbling: by these means each film is further retarded and rerouted from its ostensible goal. Or rather, by these means the true goal is revealed: goallessness and play. In *Which Way to the Front?*, all that remains to attract the man who has done everything are games of mimicry. In the boardroom scene of *The Errand Boy*, Morty takes a break from his mail-delivery rounds to do a pantomime impression of an executive issuing instructions to his underlings, to the accompaniment of Count Basie's "Blues in Hoss's Flat," which seemingly plays "in his head." (The use of music in this way—neither naturalized within the diegesis nor part of the normal work of the score but purely a function of the onscreen character's relationship with the cinematic apparatus at a privileged moment of the narrative—extends a convention of the musical film.) Languagelessness functions as a musical parody of authority and its orders, as the film enters into a state of play and bliss.

Lewis is one of the main exponents in cinema of the tradition of American Jewish verbal humor. All his films have a clear allegiance to this tradition—including *The Bellboy,* in which Lewis is silent for most of his onscreen appearances. Stanley's silence functions as the obstinate and defiant bearing of a mark of difference—a "Jewish" ironic subversion. *Which Way to the Front?* is not only the most explicitly Jewish of his films (deliriously so, in the great scene of Byers/Kesselring's meeting with Hitler) but also the one in which Lewis asserts most aggressively some of the "Jewish" aspects of his verbal art: the rough, braying timbres intended to grate, the broken rhythms and musical cadences, creatively mangled syntax, an obsessional insistence on the proper name (Byers's incessant "Schroeder"s), a blatant disrespect for the tyranny and prestige of "correct" linguistic forms (see the scene in which Byers, trying to learn German from a phonograph record, is not content merely to fracture the phrases he's supposed to repeat but also mocks the punctiliousness of the instructor and the sound of the German language). Playing Byers playing Kesselring, Lewis unleashes and neutralizes the hidden violence of speech (see fig. 9).

One of the pleasures of Lewis's films is his distinctive, Yiddish-inflected reinvention of the English language. Lewis's linguistic universe is filled with gerunds. "If it's for drinking or looking—we'll make it!" proclaims the sign outside the glass factory in *Hardly Working.* "Stop with the brushing," Jerry Lewis, a VIP guest at the Fontainebleau Hotel, repeatedly tells a member of his staff in *The Bellboy.* The sequence in which this line is spoken contains several other examples of Lewis's characteristic idiom, abrupt and peremptory in inventiveness: to forestall the inevitable barrage of proffered lighters when he puts a cigarette in his mouth, Lewis declares, "I'll smoke it dry, I'll smoke it dry." His attempt to get his staff to "hold it" becomes an elaborate, parodic address built

Figure 9. The hidden violence of speech:
Paul Winchell, Dack Rambo, Jerry Lewis, John
Wood, Steve Franken, and Jan Murray
in *Which Way to the Front?*

around repetitions of that colloquialism. In *Which Way to the Front?*,
Byers dryly asks Finkel (John Wood) to report on his staff's behavior:
"Are they holding it?"

An apt general title for Lewis's cinema might be "How to Undo Things
with Words." In *The Errand Boy,* the scene in which the mailroom manager gives the clerks their assignments is full of strange locutions (starting
with the manager's introductory "Now listen, and listen loud!"), many of
them attempts to describe processes of understanding and cognition.
"Don't yell or hit," Morty begs his boss, assuring him, "I'm going to listen to every clear" and "I'll do all the things." Signifying his grasp of the
principles of mail delivery, Morty says, "If I see it says to go to a place,
I'll go *there,* but if I don't, then it'll—won't be clear." When the truculent
manager, with sublime irony or self-ignorance, calls himself "a very patient man," Morty replies, "I noticed before how terrific your mind is."
The manager goes on to give an account of his psyche: "It takes a great

deal for me to become unhinged for one reason or another. But, you see, when my nerves tip me off that I'm going to become unglued, that's when I have to assert myself, do you understand that, Morty?" Morty replies, "You're about to smack *people,* right?" The manager delivers one of those speeches, frequent in Lewis's films, in which an elaborate explicitness about emotional and psychological processes combines with an awkward lay vocabulary ("when my nerves tip me off that I'm going to become unglued" is a magnificent phrase) to produce a hilarious and weird parody of self-insight, filled with strangely distorted echoes of things picked up somewhere or other in American mass culture.

For Lewis, words are a contagion. During the rehearsal of the Copa Café monologue in *The Patsy,* Stanley, between garbled attempts at reciting the jokes that have been written for him, repeats fragments that he picks up from the reactions of his handlers ("he needs help"), who are being driven beyond their patience by his incompetence. The scene hinges on a confusion of pronouns and of identity that subverts the distribution of roles. "I'd like to introduce myself, but I don't know you either," tries Stanley, only to be corrected by an exasperated Chic: "No! No! 'Me,' it's 'me,' not 'you,' it's 'me'!" Later, when Stanley starts directing Harry (Keenan Wynn) instead of vice versa, Harry yells back, "It's not me, it's you!" Words can pass from one person to another and can occupy, indifferently, one person or another. The shot/reverse shot interplay becomes a relation of absolute otherness, indifference, and mutual rejection in which subjects and proper names are confused (as in Morty's failed attempts to learn the names Wabenlottnee and Babewosentall in *The Errand Boy*).

Lewisian speech accommodates radical contradiction: a gangster (B. S. Pully) in *The Bellboy* tells his underlings (Maxie Rosenbloom and Joe E. Ross) to kick a hole in a guy's chest, knock his brains out, and so on, concluding, "And remember one thing: no violence!" In *The Bellboy,* a young woman talking to her mother on a payphone irrelevantly produces the phrase, "Movies are your best entertainment." (Repeated in the board-meeting scene near the beginning of *The Errand Boy* and by the narrator at the end of *The Big Mouth,* the slogan originated with an industry-wide promotional campaign to boost theater attendance in the late 1930s.) Lewis sees speech as internally self-contradictory, free from the immediate situation, not tied to the speaking individual, as self-defeating as it is tautological and self-affirming. Instead of using dialogue for purposes of naturalism or narrative, Lewis and his collaborator Bill Richmond write dialogue in which speech consists of advertisements, catchphrases, and slogans. They reveal the tendency of language to program and serve stereotyped needs or to interpellate the person who is to be the bearer of the needs. The linguistic difficulties of Lewis's characters disrupt this process by making fun of it.

Lewisian Space

In *The Family Jewels,* the armored-car heist and the kids' softball game occupy two different spaces, two different worlds, separated by a fence (which Willard crawls through to retrieve a ball). Divisions, thresholds, and doors haunt and fascinate Lewis. In *The Errand Boy,* the head of the mailroom has an obsessive aversion to the sound of the door slamming. In *The Nutty Professor* and *The Family Jewels,* doors are always a problem. Miss Lemon (Kathleen Freeman), responding to a summons from Dr. Warfield at the beginning of *The Nutty Professor,* accidentally knocks him down when she opens the door to his office; a few moments later, Kelp is found underneath a door that the explosion in his classroom has turned into a coffin lid (showing that the door is an entrance into life and that life, in Lewis's cinema, is equal to being visible); still later, Kelp knocks Stella down by opening a door. In *The Family Jewels,* Willard, by opening the door to the lawyers' office, accidentally causes one of the lawyers (Jay Adler) to become attached to the door; later, opening the door to Uncle Julius's studio, Willard creates another absurd calamity; finally, he arrives at a house that has recently exploded but doesn't collapse until he knocks at the door. In *Hardly Working,* Bo, trying to leave Balling's office, first opens an overfilled closet by mistake, causing its contents to tumble out onto the floor, then finds the right door but, in his struggle to open it, pulls it out by its hinges.

If the door motif in Lewis suggests a prevailing horizontality, *The Patsy* is a highly vertical film, as the opening titles sequence announces with its special effect of Stanley apparently falling from the balcony of a hotel suite, his cutout figure matted over still photographs of the hotel. This fall (which he finishes by rebounding from a swimming-pool diving board) is reenacted at the end of the film, but this time the horizontal reasserts itself over the vertical, as Lewis opens a door in an apparent balcony wall to disclose that the space into which Stanley has just fallen is only a continuation of the floor of the set where the film is being shot.

A main principle of Lewis's films is not to fill in everything, especially the kinds of marginal or liminal spaces that conventional narrative films, to secure an impression of naturalism, generally fill in. In the astonishing overhead crane shot in Kelp's laboratory in *The Nutty Professor,* the camera reaches a distance hard to reconcile with the presumed real dimensions of the space, letting us know explicitly that this is a fantasy space, a movie set, a space of experimentation with identity. The space of *The Ladies Man* is a charged one of libidinal drives surrounded by an emptiness that Lewis pulls his camera back far enough to let us see.[6]

Lewis's compartmentalized sets facilitate the discovery of inner narratives and secret worlds. In *Which Way to the Front?,* the mini-narratives of Byers's relationships with an Italian mayor's wife (Kaye Ballard) and with Hitler take place entirely inside rooms that seal off these encounters from the rest of the castle and from the rest of the film. Within the artificial universe of the boarding house in *The Ladies Man,* Miss Cartilage's suite is a universe unto itself, with its all-white decor; it also has its own spatial laws, since it proves to contain not only Miss Cartilage's bedroom but a vast ballroom with a bandstand, on which Harry James and his big band are gathered to give a private concert (see fig. 10). Lewis reveals the ballroom with a cut that transforms not only space but costume: Herbert leaves one shot wearing his usual casual attire to emerge in the next shot wearing a snazzy suit. The Miss Cartilage sequence represents not only a private episode for Herbert, self-contained and without antecedents or consequences in the narrative, but also a dangerous encounter with the figure of Sexual Woman, from which he has been in flight since his sweetheart's traumatizing betrayal. It is, furthermore, a fantasy in which he momentarily asserts a mastery of performance (and a slick wardrobe) not revealed in the rest of the film.

The Miss Cartilage fantasy reveals Lewis's cinema as one of pure play, expressed through the control of color, decor, and camera movement in a studio environment, through dance, and through the indulgence of his love of big-band swing (a musical style that features in many Lewis films, notably *Cinderfella, The Errand Boy,* and *The Nutty Professor*).

Figure 10. *The Ladies Man:* Harry James, Jerry Lewis, and Sylvia Lewis (as Miss Cartilage).

All these elements, which Lewis's work constantly links to the free exercise of the imagination, point to a conception of film as a medium of transformation and escape, aligned with a tradition of Hollywood luxury and artistry.

The campus in *The Nutty Professor* is a volatile space of personal transformation. At the start of the film, an explosion turns the world ninety degrees on its axis and leaves behind a thick fog suggestive of the origin of life: we witness death and rebirth occurring in abstract space. The settings in the film make these processes manifest: Warfield's outsized office, which makes Kelp shrink (as Stanley shrinks beside Ellen in *The Patsy,* sitting on the ottoman she wheels out from beneath her desk) but which Love dominates and turns into an ironic and pitiless theatre; Kelp's childhood home, remembered in flashback, with its wide-angle perspectives and outsized sets and props that decrease the apparent size of the father, and, in the extreme background, Julius in the crib; the auditorium that becomes the site of a purely personal confession (and to which is adjoined a backstage area of solitude and deflation, feelings familiar to any performer and no doubt a source of particular terror to Lewis); above all, the Purple Pit, the most alluring of Lewis's escapist sites, a zone of romanticism, illusion, and alcoholic dissolution of identity.

The Purple Pit is a magic space that Love completely controls, turning it into his own stage, reflecting his moods and whims. It is a fragmented, shifting space, different in different conditions: initially it is crowded, public, bright, and splashed with color; but when Love plays "Stella by Starlight" on the piano, apparently for Stella alone, the space becomes a dark, after-hours, womblike enclosure, dominated by a black-and-white painting of a man seated at a piano in front of a Dali-like imaginary landscape in receding perspective. The space of entertainment and show business is a space for the protagonist's multiplication and reflection, mutating with his or her moods. In *Three on a Couch,* Lewis treats the space of psychiatry in a somewhat similar manner. Elizabeth's inner office is little more than a blank white wall before which the characters alone exist, a pure, stripped theater of observation. Here is Lewis's most minimal, most abstract mise-en-scène. The deliberately unrealistic studio lighting creates a privileged world apart, created and inhabited only by colored lights and by the words of the patients and their psychiatrist. Like the multicolored lights and liquids in Kelp's lab in *The Nutty Professor,* the colors in Elizabeth's office represent various aspects of people, as if a person possessed or were, alternately or at the same time, different colors. (In *The Nutty Professor,* the colored liquids with which the film opens, and which spill messily on the floor in the first transformation sequence, suggest the fragmentation of identity into various components that are being remixed.)

The characteristic Lewisian environment is luxurious, colorful, and well-appointed. Chris's living room in *Three on a Couch* is a large space with red wall-to-wall carpet, red chairs, black leather sofas, and red curtains (cf. Lord Sydney's garish bachelor pad in *One More Time*). The size of the hotel-suite set in *The Patsy* permits Lewis to isolate different color fields and different moods within it: at the beginning of the film, when the star comedian Wally Brandford has just died, the characters (dressed in dark funeral clothes) congregate near a large, black sofa; at the end of the film, after Stanley's rebirth on the *Ed Sullivan Show,* an explosion of color occurs as the characters congregate around a bright orange sofa with multicolored cushions.

Lewis uses color to generate a sense of liveliness and profusion. "Color is another part of the magic, the majesty of making films, and should be used that exact way," he writes (*Total Film-Maker* 88). *The*

Ladies Man, The Nutty Professor, and *Three on a Couch* provide the most dazzling examples of this majesty: their bright colors evoke an artificial playland of manufactured products, a consumerist paradise that becomes increasingly cloying from film to film while retaining its primary meanings of utopia and escape. One is tempted to speak of the color in these films as working directly on the viewer's sense of sight; but it would be more accurate to say that Lewis's colors, which animate the frame and evoke the atmosphere and energy of such color musicals of the 1950s as *Singin' in the Rain,* function as a sign of the possibilities of cinema and as a declaration of the function of cinema. "'The sets should be in bright colors, be luxurious, beautiful, and vast, and be worth the price of the ticket. I don't think that a man or a woman who have lived their whole lives in a two-room apartment want to spend eight dollars to watch another couple in a two-room apartment for an hour and a half. I think it's important for them to get out of their little world and to see up there on the screen something like the glamour, the fantasy, the unreachable, everything that Hollywood has done, and that the whole world is forgetting'" (qtd. in Benayoun 175). This is the other side of the Lewisian discourse on Hollywood from the critique of *The Errand Boy:* the therapeutic function of cinema. Indeed, most of Lewis's color films are concerned with healing and with happiness, whereas his two black-and-white films (*The Bellboy* and *The Errand Boy*) depict their heroes' misadventures in more external terms, so that the possibility of personal happiness arises, at best, as a mirage.

The Ladies Man, Lewis's first color film, sets color and black-and-white in conflict throughout, starting with the opening titles, whose color letters are printed in a deluxe book of black-and-white still photographs of Lewis and women in various costumes. Later in the film, black-and-white photographs appear in Katie's office and on Herbert's dresser; the TV monitor in the *Up Your Street* sequence displays a black-and-white image; and a huge black-and-white photograph of Mrs. Wellenmelon looms over the announcer Westbrook van Voorhis. Finally, there is the Miss Cartilage sequence, with its pure white decor. "The nearest I've ever been able to get to a true black-and-white is when I shot the black-and-white set in color for *The Ladies Man,*" Lewis writes, noting that "there has never been a black-and-white picture [because] it comes out in shades of gray" (*Total Film-Maker* 87). *The Bellboy* and

The Errand Boy are gray films of photographic realism, whereas *The Ladies Man, The Nutty Professor, The Patsy, The Family Jewels, Three on a Couch,* and *One More Time* are exuberant films of color stylization. In *The Ladies Man,* the black-and-white image within the color image is a representation, an acknowledged piece of manufactured imagery, or an allusion to the past. The presence of black-and-white within the color image helps foreground the constructed, multi-part nature of the photographed reality.

Lewisian space is shiny and sleek: the cinematography in *The Bellboy* enhances the otherworldly smoothness of the great expanses of floor, with their abstract decorative lines and patterns. A constant theme in Lewis is the smoothness of surfaces into which nothing can be inserted, from which nothing can be extracted, on which nothing can catch. In the gym scene in *The Nutty Professor,* Kelp can't put his glasses away because he has no pockets—a characteristic Lewis gag, reminiscent of the moment in *The Ladies Man* in which, pretending to search for a letter of reference to give to Katie, Herbert stalls by repeatedly letting his hand slide over the pockets of his jacket. In *The Bellboy,* Stanley confronts the problem of how to pick up a suitcase that has no handle. The floor of the psychiatrist's office in *Cracking Up* is so highly polished that Warren repeatedly slips on it throughout the long opening-titles sequence (later in the film he defeats this particular adversary by putting on flippers).

The opening of a film demands the vast space of an office (*The Bellboy, Cracking Up*) or hotel suite (*The Patsy*): the choice of setting emphasizes the ceremonial nature, and the arbitrariness, of the act of setting the film in motion. The largeness of the realm of the possible, within which the film will be circumscribed, translates to the space. At the beginning of *The Patsy,* the handlers, bereft of their star, ponder the emptiness—spatial and professional—before them and call for a new star to fill it. Near the beginning of *The Family Jewels,* it is once again a question of a death and a role to be filled: which of the uncles will Donna (under the terms of her father's will) choose to be her guardian? The lawyers' office, where this question is initially posed and where Willard's arrival disguised as Everett answers it at the end of the film, translates the question into spatial terms, laying out a large space of possibility on which Lewis's film writes itself. The sequence of Chris's acceptance of the prize in *Three on a Couch* directly recalls the ending of *The Family Jewels:* the vast official space revealed in a wide shot, with the Lewis character arriving to present himself.

The Bellboy, a film about enclosure, constantly makes its home in vast spaces: the hotel auditorium where Stanley must set up chairs for a movie show, the sky (in the scene of Stanley's improvisatory airplane flight and the scene in which the pop of his flash bulb changes night to day), the golf course, the race track. These are all spaces too big for humanity that Stanley domesticates by establishing relations with specific, small objects: the single chair he places so painstakingly in the middle of a vast empty space at the outset of his Herculean task (see fig. 11), the briefcase he fetches from the plane, the camera and its flash, the dogs. Denying his own solitude, which these huge spaces heighten, he fills their immensity with music (the conducting scene), characters, sounds, and light. Solitude becomes a theme again in *The Errand Boy,* with its shots of Morty alone: the long shot of him sauntering into a soundstage with a swimming pool, or at the large table in the chairman's office, doing his pantomime routine to "Blues in Hoss's Flat." The gradual revelation of the size of the set (and in particular the large table) at the beginning of the latter scene is a crucial gesture (repeating, on a smaller scale, the withdrawal of the camera before the dollhouse set of *The Ladies Man*): a crane shot shows Morty entering the office, putting papers on

Figure 11. Jerry Lewis in *The Bellboy.*

the desk at the back of the set, then walking forward to the table (the camera craning back as he does so) and sitting down.

At the end of the scene in *The Bellboy* in which Stanley conducts an invisible (but audible) orchestra, the unexpected sound of applause is accompanied by an equally unexpected light change: the house lights dim, with a spotlight shining on Stanley. Similarly, in *The Ladies Man*, in the high-angle shot of Herbert dancing with George Raft (a scene that could be Herbert's fantasy, just as the conducting scene is Stanley's), lights go down on the house set and a follow spot goes up on Raft and Herbert. Filmic space in Lewis's films merges with performance space and becomes theatricalized. Making his singing debut at the Purple Pit in *The Nutty Professor*, Love controls the environment by demanding "sexy" lighting. At the beginning of *Which Way to the Front?*, a light change accompanies the drastic switch from a naturalistic narrative scene to a parodic patriotic speech addressed toward the camera by Byers ("In a democracy, it's every man's right to be killed fighting for his country"), while his staff line up behind him to hum "America the Beautiful." Near the end of "In Dreams They Run," the muscular-dystrophy sufferer Davey is deposited in the foreground of a wide shot and left to ponder whether he will finally accept the wheelchair that his doctors have recommended for him and that looms behind him in the middle of the composition: at this point, an unmotivated, unnaturalized dimming of the lights in the foreground emphasizes not just the importance of the mental and emotional processes going on within him but also their private, inaccessible nature.

With the mediatization of the house in *The Ladies Man* comes the total conflation of domestic and performance spaces. At the start of the breakfast sequence, as the women do their morning exercises, put on makeup, and so on, they are on full display and seem to be performing for the audience on the other side of the dollhouse's absent fourth wall. In a logical transformation, the house becomes a TV studio when it is invaded by the crew of the program *Up Your Street*. The division between private and public space is nonexistent throughout *The Ladies Man*; even scenes that resemble fantasies, such as Herbert's encounters with Raft and with Miss Cartilage, are staged as public performances. Lewis's universe is one of total mediatization.

"It's a movie set" (the end of *The Patsy*): a central affirmation in Lewis's work, it could be said of so many of his spaces, even the hotel in *The Bellboy.* All the world is a movie set. Lewis's films often take place in fantasy spaces, in artificial preserves, in factories (*The Errand Boy,* obviously; but also *The Ladies Man,* set in a boarding school for aspiring Hollywood starlets) and showrooms of pleasure, such as the clothing store in *Three on a Couch.* If the Paramount-backlot streets seen in Lewis's films from *The Ladies Man* to *The Family Jewels* are the simulacra of a social space, the social space itself is a simulacrum, as Lewis proves in *The Bellboy.* By shooting at the Fontainebleau, Lewis exposes the cinematic nature of the hotel and of self-claimed "reality." In *The Big Mouth, Hardly Working,* and *Cracking Up,* Lewis visits places in the so-called real world to find, again, their artifice, their constructed nature. The bank in *Cracking Up* becomes a movie set, complete with surveillance monitors that function like video-assist monitors (Lewis invented the video assist and introduced it to Hollywood with *The Bellboy*). The commercial advertisements that saturate the social space of *Hardly Working* (as in the hilarious scene in which Bo elaborately samples Frank's box of Dunkin' Donuts) subvert the logic of "product placement" to reveal the advertising nature of an entire society.

Many of the blocks of cinema of which *The Bellboy* is constructed deal with attempts to use the hotel for escape, such as the sequences involving a pair of clandestine lovers and a newlywed couple, or for personal transformation, such as the Miss Hartung sequence. Stanley, whose role throughout much of the film consists of unintentionally undermining and frustrating others' escape attempts, functions as an agent of the critique of the fantasy as commodity. Walter Winchell, in his voiceover narration at the beginning of the film, identifies Miami as a place where people come to "play" and "pay"—a motif reintroduced later when Stanley causes bright sunlight to appear at 3:30 AM by snapping a photo of the moon, whereupon a guest is heard to say, "For the money it's costing, we'll take the sun whenever they give it to us"—as if the sun itself were a commodity. (Stanley, like other Lewis characters, also becomes the privileged subject of a private, noncommodified fantasy, which Lewis-as-director shares with the audience—notably in the sequence of the invisible orchestra.)

Lewis's America belongs partly to fantasy and partly to documentary. The San Diego resort area in *The Big Mouth* really exists and is filmed accordingly, but it becomes a fantasy of itself—an aspect of the film that is highlighted by the cameo appearance of Colonel Sanders of

Kentucky Fried Chicken fame as an irascible hotel guest. The intrusion of the narrative into the near-science-fiction spaces of Sea World, including the moment when, escaping from his pursuers, Clamson disguises himself and takes part in a kabuki performance, further heightens this fantasy aspect. *The Big Mouth* belongs to a tradition of film comedies set at resorts. In such films, which include *Les vacances de M. Hulot, The Cure,* and Lewis's own *The Bellboy* (to which *The Big Mouth* is a kind of sequel), the pursuit and supply of pleasures are typically major themes. Extending this tradition to the fragmented United States of the late 1960s, *The Big Mouth* takes place in an endzone landscape of sealed-off delusions and unpredictable sympathies and antipathies, where the futility of trying to communicate with other individuals or with society at large becomes inescapable and where, denied recognition for his experiences and perceptions, the individual is reduced to trying to erase himself.

Further down the historical line, the Florida of *Hardly Working* is a stagnant place, neither paradise nor dystopia, all too recognizable as part of the declined, post–Bretton Woods United States of the early 1980s. The film is poised awkwardly between documentary and fiction, and, as with other Lewis films, many of its scenes are either not clearly intended to be funny or are handled in such a way that their being funny or not is beside the point, since the scenes function primarily as evidence of a way of life. Most of the characters and situations of *Hardly Working* are, even though played broadly, thoroughly embedded within an implied social reality; only Lewis's character, Bo, appears not to belong to this reality and even contradicts it by his presence.

Lewis's documentation of automotive culture through several films (*The Bellboy, The Errand Boy, The Family Jewels, Hardly Working*) marks him as one of the major pop-modernists of American cinema, along with Howard Hawks, Frank Tashlin, and Andy Warhol. The tracking shot of the car wash in *The Errand Boy* celebrates the sleekness of modernity, aligning the film with some of the major themes of American pop culture (see also the parody rock song "I Lost My Heart in a Drive-in Movie" in *The Patsy*). No less than his compartmentalized block structures and his bright colors, the frequent appearance of flattened and one-dimensional visual forms in Lewis's work expresses his pop sensibility. These forms also belong to his materialism and show his insistence on the essential properties of the image, those that constitute the image as image. Again and again in Lewis's films we find revealed, at the center of a more or less rich fictional diegesis, the photographed and printed image, linking the cinematic scene to photography, especially as used in mass media: the photo album in the credits sequence of *The Ladies Man,* or the gallery of glamour photos outside Uncle Julius's studio in *The Family Jewels.* Photography doesn't preserve the world but betrays and violates it. The snapping of a photo may become an act of subversion: in *The Bellboy,* Stanley effects two of his biggest disruptions (his faux pas at the golf tournament and the night-to-day jump cut) through photography. In *The Family Jewels,* Julius's attempt to conduct simultaneously two different advertising-photo sessions turns into a typically Lewisian semi-inadvertent campaign of revenge against the smooth perfection of the models.

The image has sides that face in different directions (in the *Up Your Street* sequence in *The Ladies Man,* the small TV monitor showing a close-up of Westbrook van Voorhis faces toward us in the foreground, while the man himself is in profile in the background); the image has folds (like the fold in the middle of the double-page spreads of the credits book at the beginning of the film), lines, and partitions (the descending wall in Miss Cartilage's suite). The image is a composite. It is not always clear how to read such an image, in what order its different parts should be scanned. If Lewis is in the frame, usually he is the privileged figure, but this is not always the case: sometimes his demotion in the image is the point (as when, directed from offscreen to get out of the camera range during the shooting of *Up Your Street,* he creeps slowly out of the frame).

The Lewisian scene is like a room of variable dimensions whose walls can suddenly fly up and away (*The Ladies Man*), or which can open unpredictably onto incongruous spaces (the narrative of *Cracking Up,* like that of the second half of *Which Way to the Front?,* resembles a series of communicating rooms). Lewis sometimes violently confronts the unbreakable limits of the frame, as when Vince Barnett's antique car is crushed in the garage in *The Family Jewels.* The frame represents an arbitrary limit that Lewis usually respects: there are few zooms in his films, even those he made after the use of the zoom had become routine in Hollywood cinema. But he also extends the limit and reaches beyond it. In the shot that cranes back from Herbert in *The Ladies Man* to show the entirety of the dollhouse set, or the shot that cranes up from Kelp writhing on the floor of his lab in *The Nutty Professor,* Lewis contemplates the possible annulment of the fiction: the movement of the camera breaches the limit of the frame as a stable, defined site. These moments are akin to the shots that emphasize the solitude of the Lewis figure in an immense space in *The Bellboy* and *The Errand Boy:* the size of the space is only appreciable in relation to a human figure, but Lewis always pushes this relation to an extreme (as in *One More Time,* in the scene of Charlie alone in the castle).

The Frame and Its Obstructions

In *The Total Film-Maker,* Lewis writes: "In pictures I direct I do not allow any cinematographer to get behind the camera until after I position it, select the lens, set it for marks; frame high, low, left or right, and then lock it. After that, he can light. . . . I feel that the moment a director tells his cinematographer, 'This is what I'd like to see,' the director is no longer composing the shot. He abandons a creative responsibility" (89–90). *The Errand Boy* declares itself early on to be a film about the frame and what it reveals and conceals. After a short series of banal scenes from commercial films (of various genres, reminding us, as does the prologue of *The Bellboy,* that Hollywood is a cinema of genres), Lewis follows up with "behind-the-scenes" shots that reveal what lies outside the edges of the film frame and what occurs before the printed take. In one case, a person we took to be a woman, standing with her back to the camera while receiving repeated slaps from a male character, turns out to be a male stand-in (Mike Mazurki) in a woman's wig and costume. That particular gambit—concealing a face and making its revelation, when the person turns toward the camera, the punchline of the scene—occurs again later in *The Errand Boy,* when the person giving a moralizing lecture about the importance of being nice turns out to be the famously truculent baseball-team manager Leo Durocher (Milton Berle's cameo in drag in *Cracking Up* is another variation on this theme).

The widening of the field of vision becomes a metaphor for the film. It happens again near the end of *The Errand Boy:* a shot of Morty with the overflowing champagne bottle unexpectedly appears to zoom out optically; then it turns out that the scene is being projected on a screen, from which the camera is tracking back. The shock of this revelation (which recalls a central moment in Fritz Lang's final film, *Die tausend Augen des Dr. Mabuse* [The Thousand Eyes of Dr. Mabuse; 1960]) is completely logical. The frame provides security and stability and confers an internal consistency on the things it contains, but from the beginning of *The Errand Boy*, Lewis plays on the absence of something from the frame, later disclosed, that would allow us to perceive that consistency as the result of a mise-en-scène—to perceive that these things, consistent among themselves, are only surface appearances selected out of a self-contradictory reality.

Lewis does the same thing at the end of *The Patsy:* with the acknowledgment that Stanley/Lewis and Ellen/Ina Balin are actors in a film, the field of view again widens beyond the initial frame. Here, the frame is metaphorical: the set or sum of what we know ("the people in the theater know I ain't going to die," Lewis, as "himself," informs Balin). The widening of the frame also constitutes the structural point of Lewis's short film "Boy." The hero of the film is a young light-skinned boy who appears to be the victim of racial prejudice in a well-to-do community otherwise populated entirely by blacks. At the end of the film, the camera, pulling back from a close shot of the boy at the dinner table, reveals that his parents and siblings are black.

Lewis's work also manifests a recurrent need to close down and narrow the frame—to have that which signifies, acts, performs, and expresses occupy an ever-smaller part of a screen that is taken up otherwise with the inexpressive, the merely objective or object-like. In the first scene in Warfield's office in *The Nutty Professor,* a wide-angle, high-angle shot over Warfield's shoulder finds Kelp tucked into the middleground behind the angled edge of the desk. In the first hotel-suite sequence of *The Patsy,* the dark-suited backs of the handlers blot out Stanley in his individualizing red jacket. Later in the film, when Ellen kisses Stanley, the back of her dark-haired head fills the frame. In the restaurant scene, the violinists circling around the couple's table block Ellen and Stanley from our view (just as, in the next shot, the orchestra's music drowns out the sound of the couple's conversation—an example of the sound/image equivalence that is one of the principles of Lewis's cinema).

As he tries to register at the hotel in *The Bellboy,* Jerry Lewis becomes hidden from the camera by the crowding of his staff. In the morning sequence of *The Ladies Man,* in the cafeteria, Herbert is in the background, his figure blotted out by the figures of the girls. In *The Errand Boy,* the extras who line up to be marched onto a sound-stage trap Morty against a wall and block him from the camera, forcing him to squeeze his way into the line to be seen. Later in the film, as an elevator fills with people, Morty, initially alone at the back of the elevator, again becomes hidden from the view of the camera. Remaining within (and foregrounding) the logic of the star system, Lewis's art of concealment and revelation takes his own figure as that which is concealed and revealed most obsessively—even to the level of disguising the obsessiveness as an elaborate accident. The rushes of the cocktail-party scene that "the Baron" (Sig Ruman) has directed find Morty, in the background, repeatedly revealed by the movements of a foreground extra, then concealed again, and finally peeking up over the heads of the extras to look at the camera (see fig. 12). His intermittent and insistent presence disrupts the Baron's film.

In the movie-premiere sequence, Morty is initially concealed among the crowd outside the theater, only to be revealed when an extra in the foreground changes position; later, in the scene of the birthday celebration for a star, Anastasia Anastasia (Iris Adrian), Morty is at first invisible, then is belatedly revealed pushing a cart that carries a cake and

Figure 12. Jerry Lewis in *The Errand Boy.*

champagne. Shots such as these last two seem designed to arouse the viewer's curiosity as to how and where the Lewis character will appear in a scene, creating a suspense whose arbitrariness with respect to the narrative underlines a purely cinematic logic. Similarly, *Which Way to the Front?* features a composition of German officers in a room, forming a solid block on the left side of the frame, behind which Byers/Kesselring invisibly enters to place himself inconspicuously in the right background, before announcing his presence to them (and us) with his first line. The frame, for Lewis, becomes a hiding place and a three-dimensional field of overlapping surfaces and volumes. Lewis underlines the importance of his characters' comings into and goings from the frame with dialogue that makes the theme of leave-taking explicit: Herbert's long, awkward, and finally aborted farewell attempt at the end of *The Ladies Man* ("When the door slams, my life is out of yours"); Clamson warning the highway patrol officers of his intention to exit the scene in *The Big Mouth;* Bo's taking leave of Balling after creating a mess in his office in *Hardly Working* ("Okay, I'm leaving it, and I'm leaving. But this leaving is not leaving it; I mean, I'm going, but it's staying"). Going and coming are matters that Lewis takes most seriously.

Lewis's creativity with obstructive bodies reaches a peak in *Three on a Couch*. A striking composition shows Susan (Mary Ann Mobley) tucked into the upper right of the frame behind Elizabeth's back, which takes up the rest of the shot. In a later scene, Susan, during her psychiatric session, does leg exercises in the foreground while Elizabeth, at her desk, is framed between Susan's legs. *Three on a Couch* is explicitly a film about blockage and force, about the physicality of point of view. Throughout the film, the characters' problems arise out of their visual situatedness for one another in a world of illusion; as in *The Ladies Man,* the central problem is one of leaving that world, a problem expressed by Elizabeth's refusal to separate from her patients. Visibility is full of traps and blocks. Early in the film, as Chris tries to persuade Elizabeth to accompany him to Paris, Lewis plays a fairly long two-shot on his back and her face; only at the very end of the shot does Chris turn toward the camera. In a scene in Chris's apartment, the camera executes a slow circular track around the couch as Chris and Elizabeth kiss; during part of the camera's trajectory, the couple's backs are to the camera. Chris is filmed from behind again during the great dance long take, the camera apparently delegating to him, or sharing with him, its gaze at the enraptured Elizabeth (though, as the end of the shot reveals, he's been sleeping on his feet). The mise-en-scène thwarts and denies the expressiveness of faces.

In the party sequence of *Three on a Couch*, the film reaches a plateau of delirious visual excess. Everything is too much: sensory overload of music, people, and movement; the persistent annoyance of Buddy Lester's drunk. Through it all, and through the following sequence in which the partygoers pursue Chris and Elizabeth to the pier, Lewis remains concerned with the boundaries of the space—Chris clings to the edge of the space, trying to escape (via the elevator; see fig. 13)—and with things that spill over or poke through (the drunk's body partially hanging out of the window of the cab or dangling from a life preserver that is being hoisted up on a crane). As in other Lewis films, the frame is crammed with things, the way Kelp's body is crammed into the shelf in *The Nutty Professor,* the way bodies are crammed into the elevator in *The Errand Boy,* and extras are crammed into the mises-en-scène of the two German-accented directors in that same film. Space is conceived always, therefore, as a limit, a frame.

Figure 13. Visual excess in *Three on a Couch:*
James Best, Renzo Cesana, Fritz Feld,
Jerry Lewis, and Janet Leigh.

The Big Mouth reveals the same immense artistry of the organization of bodies within the frame. When Clamson is threatened by gangsters, a medium shot shows him and a gangster, facing toward the camera, framed between two other gangsters who have their backs to the camera. Lewis intercuts this shot with an off-balance close shot framing Clamson and the back of a gangster's head. The screen is a convergence of faces, arms, and weapons (the gangsters point their guns at Clamson from four directions). Clamson, pulled over on the road, is framed within the crook of the arm of a policeman who stands with his hand on his hip. Later, Clamson (in his Kelp-like disguise as a hotel guest) is framed under the hotel manager's arm, leaning on the counter. Still later, Clamson pokes his head into the shot from behind a man's leg to stare at the camera.

Stubbornly interposing themselves, people are blocks for other people and for the camera. In *Which Way to the Front?*, as in *The Big Mouth*, the proportion of space in the frame occupied by a character stands for that character's power, while the other characters must maneuver to be seen by the camera: in the foreground, the back of the head of the recruiting officer partly obstructs Byers, who is facing the camera; during the dialogue, Bland, Hackle, and Love (Dack Rambo) poke their heads into the composition in the background, peeking into the shot.

Such moments, in which Lewis plays on and foregrounds the arbitrariness of framing by adjusting the composition before the viewer's eyes, are frequent in his films. In the poolroom scene of *The Family Jewels*, the pool players stick their heads into the shot from behind foreground figures to stare at Skylock's money. In *The Patsy*, a camera movement reframes the shot of Stanley trying on a jacket in the mirror at Sy Devore's shop so that the reflection of another customer, George Raft, becomes visible (to Stanley and to the viewer): a purely optical moment. The composition may be arbitrary in relation to the face and the body: in *The Nutty Professor*, the frame cuts off the top of the head of a very tall man (Richard Kiel), then frames a second man correctly but leaves Kelp low in the frame. In the shot of Faith and her lover kissing in *The Ladies Man*, the frame neatly lops both their heads off.

Though the narrative framework is looser than in some earlier Lewis films, the visual framing in *Hardly Working* is anything but casual. A shot of Bo in a lawn chair reading a newspaper is angled so that, deep in the background, Millie appears on the tennis court in the upper half of the frame, while the empty chair beside him is balanced in the frame with him. The empty area beside Bo seems to summon Millie to occupy it, which she will shortly do. The post office scenes are a series of modernist shots with Mondrian-like compositions of boxes, file cabinets, and mail-sorting compartments—all of which Bo disrupts.

Lewis's art of the frame sometimes takes the form of grand arabesques like the opening of *The Ladies Man,* in which the camera surveys in a meticulous long take the chain of random interactions that upsets the "nervous little community" of Milltown. In *The Family Jewels,* Willard's leadership of the parade marchers (in a scene that takes off from the "Face the Music" number in Taurog's *You're Never Too Young*) promotes a beautifully stylized chaos. In *The Errand Boy,* a cutaway scene of Morty driving a trolley around the Paramutual lot implies the extent of the chaos he has been spreading. Disaster is necessary and salutary: this is a tradition in American comedy. It can break out at any moment, on any pretext (and can be summoned by the very fear of disaster, as the opening sequence of *The Ladies Man* suggests). Lewis's comedy follows this tradition by targeting all forms of repression and control and declaring them to be doomed to fail, showing their weakness before the powerful currents that will inevitably break through them. Chaos in Lewis's films also figures as a (usually indirect) form of revenge. For example, in *The Ladies Man,* Herbert's seemingly inadvertent destruction of Gainsborough's hat is a way of getting even with the man for his arrogant bullying, and in *The Nutty Professor,* Love's humiliation of Warfield obliquely avenges Warfield's treatment of Kelp. In *The Big Mouth,* Colonel Sanders's humiliation of the hotel manager avenges, indirectly, the manager's meanness to Clamson—revenge is effective as such even if it is not performed by the person being avenged. This is also the case with the comeuppances delivered to such figures as Quimby (Ray Walston) in *Who's Minding the Store?* and Tuffington (Everett Sloane) in *The Disorderly Orderly.*

No less than a therapeutic expedient or an ideological device, disaster for Lewis is a structural imperative. In the party sequences that elaborately close *Three on a Couch,* Buddy Lester's drunk appears from out of nowhere to introduce an external element of disorder in a mise-en-scène already overloaded with elements and full of strain. The catastrophes unleashed by Lewis's characters often have an outsize, excessive quality and, at the same time, are often only weakly related to his own agency. These observations find their ultimate object in his last two films with Tashlin, *Who's Minding the Store?* and *The Disorderly Orderly,* rather than in Lewis's own films—Tashlinian disaster is transhuman and universal, whereas Lewisian disaster is contained and concentrated. In *The Errand Boy,* by tripping over a garbage can, Morty causes a (naturalistically improbable) chain reaction of all the stenographers dropping piles of paper from their desks. At the end of the scene of the music lesson in *The Patsy,* the agonized Mueller's high note causes, inexplicably, the complete destruction of the set, surveyed in a long shot. What is most striking is, as usual with Lewis, a dichotomy, a split, an ambivalence: on the one hand, the loose sprawl of chaos, and on the other hand, the fanatical control of a mise-en-scène that organizes and brings forth an effect of chaos. Lewis finds the perfect image for this constant duality in *The Errand Boy:* the unintegrated, random element that sticks out because it has not been planned (Morty destroying the Baron's mise-en-scène of the party scene) has, of course, been placed there (by the true director, Lewis) so that it cannot be missed.

Disorder, for Lewis, represents social failure, whereas for Tashlin disorder is cosmic vengeance. Even when it appears (as in the Lewis scenes just mentioned) in its positive aspect as a rejection of oppressive values, social failure needs to be paired with its opposite, mastery. *The Patsy* follows a trajectory from chaos to order: from the recording studio (the forest of microphones; the A&R man yelling tonelessly) to the perfectly staged and executed *Ed Sullivan Show* skit (which, repeating the overall narrative movement, concerns the hero's magical self-reinvention). *The Patsy* is the most fully achieved of Lewis's films; no scene in Lewis is more meticulously directed than the flashback high-school hop scene, which completes its own emblematic and self-contained movement from chaos to order, as, over the course of their dance, Stanley and his dancing partner change from awkwardness to grace (a triumph celebrated by the camera's graceful crane upward). In the deliriously reductive and self-reflexive ending of *The Patsy,* the exercise of directorial control for its own sake—for the sheer exhilaration of it—proves to be the point of the film.

Lewisian Time

The house that explodes from within in *The Family Jewels* doesn't collapse until Willard comes to knock at the door. In *The Errand Boy*, the suits of armor that Morty accidentally knocks over remain immobile on the ground for some time before they slowly start picking themselves up. In *The Ladies Man*, Herbert, asked by a TV soundman (Doodles Weaver) to test a microphone, shouts into it, with a predictably devastating effect on the headphones-wearing technician; the camera stays on Herbert for an extended time as he goes downstairs and looks for the soundman, who turns out to have somehow buried himself under the cushions of a sofa. When the soundman gets his revenge by yelling into the microphone while Herbert is wearing the headphones, Herbert calmly walks away before abruptly exclaiming, "Oh!" and collapsing to the floor. In this sequence, Lewis inverts the usual relationship of the components of the gag, making delay the source of the humor and the point of the joke; the punchline is merely a kind of formal obligation or punctuation.

In an original variation of Lewis's conceptual humor, sometimes he elides the punchline or payoff entirely. Usually, when there is delay in a film, we are made aware that we are waiting for something, and we know roughly what we are waiting for, but Lewis may give us the delay and then omit the predictable payoff. In *The Bellboy*, we are left to imagine what the reaction of a guest will be when he finds that the trousers he sent Stanley to press have been returned to him stiff as a board. In the swimming-pool scene of *The Errand Boy*, the introductory long shot with the pool in the foreground and Morty entering in the far background is enough to establish the inevitability of his eventual fall into the pool. Lewis cuts from Morty peering into the pool to an underwater shot of an outfitted diver at the pool bottom; then, after a moment, Morty swims into the shot. The expected gag shot, showing Morty falling into the pool, is missing. In *Hardly Working*, Bo's visit to a glass factory to apply for a job results in a dialogue-free scene comprising three shots in the company's parking lot, over which the sound of glass shattering proceeds for several seconds before Bo emerges from the building. The punchline is built into the structure of the scene and begins and ends with it: is it still a punchline?

The delayed punchline is related to the classic "slow burn" of American comedy (among its masters was Edgar Kennedy, a frequent foil for Laurel and Hardy), a device that Lewis made the principle of some of his greatest scenes, including the Buddy Lester hat scene in *The Ladies Man.* Over the course of a lengthy shot in *The Bellboy,* the hotel manager learns on the phone that Stanley has taken off in an airplane: the humor is in the extended period of calm before the actor's broad reaction ("He . . . WHAT!?") when the magnitude of Stanley's act sinks in. (Lewis re-creates the shot in *Hardly Working.*) Lewis often pushes the device past the point where it could be expected to yield laughter, as if he were testing himself (and his audience) to see how long he can make the delay last. After Clamson escapes from Fong's laboratory in *The Big Mouth,* the crooks stand in silence for several seconds before tacitly agreeing to acknowledge that their prey has left and belatedly exploding in rage—a group slow burn.

Lewis's work aggravates the psychological tension on which the slow burn is based. The scene with the music teacher in *The Patsy* is built on an unrealistic extension in duration of hyperrealistic attitudes of embarrassment, awkwardness, and polite restraint (Professor Mueller's reactions as he forbears from stopping Stanley from going around the room and touching everything). A psychological improbability—the lack of development—is built into the structure of the scene, creating awkwardness and anxiety. In the scene of the crooks' delayed reaction to Clamson's exit in *The Big Mouth,* the actors must try to fill up a mysterious space of doing nothing, and this testing of their resourcefulness creates tension. A lengthy silence precedes the first line in *Which Way to the Front?,* as Finkel stands at awkward attendance beside his boss's chair, before finally venturing: "New business to tackle, Mr. Byers?" (as if the film, barely started, were still waiting for some invisible signal from its onscreen director before it can begin in earnest). In *The Nutty Professor,* the scene of Kelp in Warfield's office starts with an extreme and awkward delay, as Warfield stares stonily at his guest, who, not knowing what to do, occupies himself with various objects.

By prolonging duration, Lewis highlights changes in behavior over a single shot or scene. Jerry Lewis and his entourage in *The Bellboy* are at the registration desk: at an arbitrary point in this long take, but not before, the entourage starts laughing at everything the star says. Here is the open revelation of structure itself, of the principle at work within the block of movements and affects that is the scene. In *The Ladies Man,* the behavior and character of Gainsborough change radically over the course of the hat scene: the turning point is Herbert's replacing the mangled hat on Gainsborough's head, whereupon the gangster-like tough instantly turns insecure and shrinks. Later in the film, George Raft, at first self-assured, becomes suddenly desperate to prove his identity (which Herbert doubts) by dancing with Herbert. In all these cases, Lewis allows the structuring principle of a scene to declare itself in a manner that is at least weakly motivated, if not totally unmotivated.

In his experiments with extended duration, Lewis is a materialist filmmaker, directing the audience's attention to the various elements of image and sound of which the scene, the block, is composed and letting them be exhaustively enumerated. Delay is a mode of confrontation: what is before the camera becomes more inescapable and more stubborn the more it is lingered on. As Raymond Durgnat notes of *The Ladies Man,* a film whose entirety he describes as a *"temps-mort,"* "The absence of continuous dramatic thread piles a special intensity of audience attention on to a gag, and on to its build-up, which permit more sophisticated forms" (236). Throughout his work, Lewis stretches moments out, repeats them, indulges them, and lives in them for themselves. Lewis has no qualms about lengthening a gag through repetition, as in the scene in *The Bellboy* in which Stanley waits for an elevator that won't come, all the while banging on the buttons and the door and making gestures of helplessness in the direction of the bell captain, who (embodying another principle of Lewisian comedy, the unresponsive partner) stands watching stonily. In *One More Time,* the slowness of a butler carrying the dinner tray to the table occasions a bizarrely protracted series of surreal visual gags, as Chris and Charlie apparently age several years while waiting for their meal (a more muted variation on this idea occurs in the superb restaurant sequence in *Cracking Up*).

The Big Mouth is full of pauses and longueurs; the principles of the narrative are interruption, fixation, and forgetting the point (the diamonds—the pretext for the plot and the motive for the actions of Thor and his gang—are never found). The film has a great deal of movement, climaxing in the chase on foot through Sea World, but the narrative movement is so retarded and so indefinite that the film could be said to move backward. At one point, Clamson is pulled over by a highway patrolman, whereupon a group of other policemen gradually gather at the scene to debate the code number of Clamson's violation. The principle of this scene of splendid stasis is merely addition/subtraction: the accumulation within the frame of more and more policemen and the departure from the frame, unnoticed by them, of Clamson. Later in the film, Clamson's encounter with Webster, the supposed FBI man, in the hotel restaurant not only fails to advance the plot, it brings it to a standstill.

The mail-delivery sequence in *The Ladies Man*, with Herbert becoming embroiled in a series of encounters with the women of the house as he delivers each one her mail, exemplifies an important aspect of duration in Lewis's work: seriality. The house set itself, with its separate and equivalent apartments, is a serial construction. Lewis often builds sequences in terms of repetitive series—of people in a line, for instance. When Jerry Lewis arrives at the hotel in *The Bellboy*, a protracted take shows an impossibly long series of members of his entourage leaving the limousine, until (after the camera executes a graceful crane shot across the top of the car) the star himself makes his long-awaited appearance at the end of the line. In *The Errand Boy*, a group of people file past Morty out of the office he is trying to enter. Similarly, in a magnificent scene in *The Nutty Professor*, Stella, still dazed by her last night's encounter with the mysterious Buddy Love, must wait at the open classroom doorway (before the eyes of the transfixed Kelp, who imagines her in successive costumes) while a long series of students files in. A variation on this idea is the succession of female models who walk past Ringo in the store in *Three on a Couch*.

In the scenes in *The Nutty Professor* and *Three on a Couch*, it is as if Lewis were unable to conceive of desire without also immediately conceiving of the multiple. The desired object is not desired alone; it exists in a profusion that is expressed as a series. Or rather, desire itself leads to a state of multiple vision in which the object appears as a repetition of itself. The trouble that desire usually causes for Lewis's characters is expressed no less through this multiplicity (as with the convention of models in *The Bellboy* and the female boarders in *The Ladies Man*) than through its standardization, which paradoxically renders the desired object at once more available and more elusive.

(In *The Family Jewels*, Willard is lost in daydreams before the gallery of glamour photos outside Julius's studio.) Always, the multiple is a value of time, whether the items appear across the scene in succession, like the models in *Three on a Couch*, or all at once, like the models in *The Bellboy* or the group of women who attend Chris's funeral in *One More Time*, identically dressed in black veils and black leather miniskirts. The screen becomes a space of desire in which desire is expressed in terms of duration.

In the swimming-pool scene in *The Errand Boy*, as Morty approaches the camera from the distant background, depth is the visual correlative of the duration of the shot. *The Bellboy*, too, is a film of extreme depth of field. In a wide-angle shot of the empty ballroom that he must fill with chairs, Stanley enters from behind the camera and walks all the way to the back of the room, becoming tiny. A composition with four bellboys in medium shot shows the dog-track field and scoreboard in clear focus in the distant background. Stanley, in the foreground of another shot, watches "Stan Laurel" go all the way to the back of the set and get into an elevator. The final shot of *The Bellboy* has Stanley, in the hotel lobby, walking away from the camera into the background. Translating time into space, these shots create passageways of infinite time, extending the possibilities (already enlarged by the Lewisian block structure) for time to move through the film.

Lewis also relates time to space by emphasizing the pause before a place is filled. At the beginning of *The Bellboy*, Stanley is missing from his place in line, and then he pops into it. Herbert's introduction at the graduation ceremony in *The Ladies Man* is based on a similar idea: the Lewis character is at first absent from a large block of people sitting in the auditorium, in whose midst he suddenly emerges, leaping into the air like a jack-in-the-box when the speaker on stage mentions his name.

In the scene of Stanley's stand-up debut at the Copa Café in *The Patsy*, humor arises from the confrontation of two deficiencies: the lack of response from the sparse audience, and Stanley's lack of performance skill. Lewis emphasizes both lacks by drawing out the scene through a series of repetitions: Stanley's mishaps with the microphone, his botched attempts at jokes, and so on. Given a sequence that is built on the impossibility of development (since Stanley never gets better, and the audience is never amused), Lewis ends it with an arbitrary recourse to fantasy:

the image of Ellen and the handlers transformed into a firing squad (in military uniforms) to execute Stanley. The fantasy only highlights the stagnancy of a situation that, lacking a logically necessary conclusion or an internal movement that would impel it to reach one, can only be ended abruptly from outside. The fantasy image has, moreover, that peculiarly isolated quality that is characteristic of the images in Lewis's films and that marks their independence from verisimilitude and from the flow of normal storytelling.

Sound

When Donna repeats Bugsy's math lesson in *The Family Jewels*, she reproduces not only the words that Bugsy speaks but his vocal rendition of them: the reproduction is, in fact, mechanical, the tape of Bugsy's (Lewis's) voice being replayed on the soundtrack over the image of Donna. This is one of the conceptual jokes that abound in Lewis's films—a joke whose levels are uncertain, so that it's not clear what we're supposed to be laughing at. Does the humor lie in Donna's uncanny and unexpected ability to reproduce Bugsy's voice with total accuracy? Or is it a joke on the confusion between a tape recording and actual speech—a joke that would thus appeal to our knowledge that it *is* a tape recording, a knowledge from outside the diegesis (where Donna does not have a tape recorder to record and replay her uncle's speech)? The Lewisian flavor of the joke comes from the superimposition of the two possible ways of getting it, from the refusal of the film to privilege one or the other level and to reduce the ambiguity that arises from their co-presence.

No less significant in this joke is the foregrounding of recording technology. Recording is a key Lewisian obsession, in his films and in his life. Robert Benayoun, interviewing Lewis for the first of many times, was surprised to see Lewis switch on his own tape recorder: "[H]e records all his conversations, of which he keeps catalogued and numbered copies among his collections of personal scrapbooks, scripts, records, and kinescopes" (62). When I interviewed Lewis for this book, he kept his own minidisc recorder running all the time, opposite mine. Carried over into his films, the possibility granted by recording technology of multiplying and repeating lived moments becomes a highly individual manner of exploding filmic time and increasing the distance between time as filmed and time as lived. Ticklish Stanley, in the barber's chair in *The Patsy*, giggles in a fast-motion, tape-speeded-up voice. In the car wash in *The Errand Boy*, the drenched Mrs. Paramutual (Kathleen Freeman) leaks tape-reversed speech. Tape manipulation garbles both Willard's commands to the marchers in *The Family Jewels* and Studs's voice in the hospital in *The Big Mouth* (as with Mrs. Paramutual, the disruption of the character's voice is the direct result of a disastrous contact with the Lewis figure).

In each of these scenes, a certain brutality can be felt in the way the film takes over the character's voice and separates it from the image of the character, visibly and audibly subjecting the character to a mechanical process, violating the (imaginary) integrity of the person. The person becomes split and recomposed, a set of components that can be independently manipulated. This process belongs to the cinematic apparatus—a prime concern of Lewis's cinema. Lewis shows how it works in the dubbing-session scene in *The Errand Boy*, in which a singer substitutes her trained voice for that of the talentless starlet singing "Lover" onscreen. This scene apparently draws its inspiration from *Singin' in the Rain*, a constant reference point for Lewis, as he proves again with the boat-captain sequence in *The Family Jewels*. In the dubbing scene in *The Errand Boy*, Lewis reverses the customary filmmaking procedure, demonstrated not only in *Singin' in the Rain* but also in *The Patsy*, of first recording the song as it is to be heard in the film and then photographing the actor lip-synching to a playback of the song. Lewis's films break the link between voice and person that is the customary guarantee of authenticity, integrity, and legitimacy. In *The Nutty Professor*, the voices of Kelp and Love emerge, inopportunely, from the mouths of each alter ego. In the record-show sequence of *The Patsy*, as in the scene of the premiere of the musical in *The Errand Boy*, bad synchronization between image and sound renders the cinematic person incoherent.

Lewis's use of sound portrays the person as a machine, on a level with the other sound-emitting devices that proliferate in his films. Miss Cartilage inaugurates the Harry James fantasy in *The Ladies Man* by placing the needle on a phonograph record. In *The Patsy*, Ferguson listens to an open-reel recording of Stanley's stand-up routine. In *The Family Jewels*, Willard, after sending Donna to bed in their hotel suite, plays a record of Gary Lewis and the Playboys' "This Diamond Ring" on the phonograph. In *Which Way to the Front?*, Byers tries to learn German from a record. The elaborate decor of the psychiatrist's office in *Cracking Up* includes a turntable.

Noise renders the human an appendage of the mechanical. Morty, on his mail-delivery run in *The Errand Boy*, enters the stenographic department to be confronted by a cacophony of typewriter noise, over which he tries without success to make his voice heard. Just as in *The Bellboy*, Jerry Lewis signals for silence from his noisy mob of assistants and hangers-on and instantly obtains it (see fig. 14), here a stenographer raises her hand, suddenly bringing the typewriters to total silence. Morty continues talking at a loud volume, but it is only nonsense, since he assumes he is still not being heard; realizing that the competing noise has stopped, he lowers his voice. This performance touch—an action painting in sound illustrating the Bergsonian definition of the comic as "du mécanique plaqué sur du vivant"—resembles the moment in *The Patsy* in which Stanley, backstage at the TV record show, can't stop dancing even though he has become aware of Ellen watching him—a moment that in turn recalls Kelp continuing to dance by himself at the prom even after he becomes aware of Dr. Warfield's disapproval.

Lewis uses sound as a weapon that acts on and overwhelms the visual field of the film and the objects in it. In *The Patsy*, as Professor Mueller

Figure 14. Lewis signals for silence in *The Bellboy*.

gets ready to produce the loud note that will disarrange Stanley's eyebrows, the sound of his preliminary intake of breath is artificially exaggerated. Later in the same sequence, Mueller's singing voice (and not, as might be expected, Stanley's bumbling) proves the destructive force that reduces his apartment to rubble. In *The Ladies Man*, headphone amplification of loud voices causes the hapless soundman to become buried under the cushions of a sofa and, later, shatters his glasses. In *The Errand Boy*, the mailroom manager's shouts and desk banging send Morty into anguished paroxysms of flinching and reeling. The scene that pushes this aspect of Lewis's work the furthest is the scene of Kelp's hangover in *The Nutty Professor*, in which sounds arising naturally out of the realistic representation of the classroom setting (chalk scraping on a chalkboard, drops of liquid falling into a test tube, a girl blowing her nose) become amplified and distorted.

Dissociated from an onscreen character's perception, the same principle of sound magnification is at work throughout Lewis's cinema. Many Lewis gags rely on combining a small sound source with a big sound: portable radios in *The Ladies Man* and *The Errand Boy*, "Baby" (the ferocious animal that roars from offscreen like a big cat but turns out to be a small dog) in *The Ladies Man*, Kelp's pocket watch in *The Nutty Professor*. In *The Family Jewels*, the sound of Matson's hand rustling inside a bag of nuts is magnified on the sound track as Skylock lines up a pool shot—an effect that recalls the click of Stanley's camera at the golf tournament in *The Bellboy*.

Despite such effects of incommensurateness, Lewis's cinema demands the equivalence of sound and image; when a sound source is no longer visible in the image, its associated sound is no longer heard. In *The Bellboy*, Stanley, covering the lens with his hand, simultaneously cuts off the babble of the female models on the soundtrack. During the mail-delivery sequence of *The Ladies Man*, a girl listening to dance music on a portable radio leaves the frame in the background by turning a corner, and the music leaves the soundtrack at the same time. In *The Errand Boy*, Morty's portable radio, loudly blaring big-band jazz in the mailroom, cannot be extinguished despite his best efforts, until he goes out the screen door with it, whereupon the sound quickly fades. The most radical sound effect in Lewis's work is the complete cutoff of sound during the TV-show scene in *The Ladies Man*, when Herbert disconnects Mrs. Wellenmelon's microphone (see fig. 15). Lewis, in his interview with me, commented: "I just included the audience into that scene. That's really going through the fourth wall." The sudden loss of sound splits the perspective of the scene in mid-take, so that we see it from one point of view but hear it (or, rather, don't hear it) from another.

His sound materialism drives Lewis to preserve and draw attention to recording mishaps and, more generally, mechanical and electronic noises that are normally suppressed in favor of a polished sound recording. Stanley starts his Copa Café monologue in *The Patsy* off-mic. As he struggles to set the mic up on its stand, the resulting noise fills the soundtrack. In the prom sequence in *The Nutty Professor*, the prominent noise of Kelp's breath on the microphone intensifies the awkwardness of his confession on stage. Near the end of the Miss Cartilage scene in *The Ladies Man*, after the Harry James song ends, we hear the crackling sound of the phonograph needle repeatedly going over the locked groove at the end of the record—a sound effect rarely used in films. In *The Errand Boy*, the tape of the fanfare at Anastasia's birthday celebration is edited so that it is prolonged in a loop, suspending the participants in a waiting to begin.

Lewis's films link music directly to fantasy. *Cinderfella* announces the crucial importance of this nexus when Lewis's Fella makes his

Figure 15. The disconnected microphone
in *The Ladies Man:* Jerry Lewis, Helen Traubel.

debut as the prince to the accompaniment of Count Basie and his big band. The conducting sequence in *The Bellboy,* the George Raft and Harry James scenes in *The Ladies Man,* the "Blues in Hoss's Flat" pantomime in *The Errand Boy,* and the high-school hop sequence in *The Patsy* are all moments in which the Lewis character frees himself from his tasks and frustrations to become the central figure in a fantasy scored with lush orchestral music. Acquiring the magical ability to sing and play the piano, Kelp as Love in *The Nutty Professor* succeeds in externalizing a fantasy self-image. The polished and swaggering big-band scores of *Three on a Couch, The Big Mouth, Which Way to the Front?,* and *Cracking Up* hold out the promise of a fusion of the fragmented identities into which the Lewis character divides in these narratives. By giving that elusive cohesion the color of a musical style that was already obsolete, or at least "dated," at the time of the earliest of these films, the scores invoke the past as a locus of continuity and plenitude. The absence of this kind of music in *Hardly Working* heightens the fretfulness and lugubriousness of that film, in which more modern pop-music styles (in the strip club scene and the disco fantasy scene) characterize a musical environment that the Lewis figure is no longer able to dominate and that fails to resonate with his own past, or that he can control only in a daydream from which he is humiliatingly awakened (as at the end of the disco fantasy).

Lewis realized at an early age that "with the voice God had given me, I certainly wasn't going to be a singer like my dad, with his Al Jolson baritone" (Lewis and Kaplan 13). This realization inspired Lewis to base his stage routine on pantomiming to records, asserting a parodic ownership of the mass-reproduced voice. With Dean Martin, Lewis liberated his own voice (accentuating its adenoidal, adolescent quality) and found a use for it as an instrument of comic retaliation and disruption. In a further development, Lewis's growing ambition and mastery led him to present himself as a legitimate singer on a series of albums starting with 1957's *Jerry Lewis Just Sings* (on which he recorded several songs associated with Jolson) and in the early solo films *The Delicate Delinquent, Rock-a-Bye Baby,* and *Cinderfella.*

The role of the voice in Lewis's self-directed films is crucial. As Scott Bukatman observes, "*The Errand Boy* is strikingly organized around the sound of the human voice, and vocal repetitions and misrepetitions determine the structure of its comedy" (194). Murray Pomerance has devoted an extended analysis to Morty Tashman's "weak vocality" and linguistic incompetence ("Errant Boy"). If the familiar childlike tones of Lewis's *shlemiel* figures (such as Morty in *The Errand Boy* and Stanley in *The Patsy*) often come to mind first in thinking of Lewis, his more flamboyant and excessive vocal characterizations, no less than his ability to use his "normal" voice for a variety of cinematic purposes, are also striking. The strident Kesselring (as himself and as impersonated by Byers) in *Which Way to the Front?*, the croaking Kelp in *The Nutty Professor* (whose tentative diction and creaky timbre are reprised by Julius in *The Family Jewels* and the disguised Clamson in *The Big Mouth*), and the simpering Rutherford in *Three on a Couch* are key examples of Lewisian figures whose vocal eccentricities permit him to foreground linguistic breakdown as performance and to make speech the main action and theme of his films, displacing narrative conflict and character development. The silence of Stanley in *The Bellboy*—less a refusal to speak than a radical, personal form of speech—is the more significant because of Lewis's vocal prowess and emphasis on speech elsewhere. Lewis's gestures toward silent cinema in the film are not only homages to particular comics (especially Stan Laurel); they are homages to the mystery and efficacy of silence itself.

The Total Filmmaker

"Literature," Maurice Blanchot writes,

> is made up of different stages which are distinct from one another and in opposition to one another. . . . The writer is not simply one of these stages to the exclusion of the others, nor is he even all of them put together in their unimportant succession, but the action which brings them together and unifies them. . . . Every time a writer is challenged in one of his aspects he has no choice but to present himself as someone else, and when addressed as the author of a beautiful work, disown that work, and when admired as an inspiration and a genius, see in himself only application and hard work, and when read by everyone, say: "Who can read me? I haven't written anything." This shifting on the part of the writer makes him into someone who is perpetually absent, an irresponsible character without a conscience, but this shifting

also forms the extent of his presence, of his risks and his responsibility. ("Literature" 368–69)

It may seem disingenuous or paradoxical to claim of someone who managed to make himself a dominant force in many media—mass media, at that—that he is like a writer "who is perpetually absent." Has not Jerry Lewis, on the contrary, made himself perpetually present? Yet no one could understand better than Lewis the "shifting" of which Blanchot writes. He has made this shifting the stance and the subject of his films: films that denounce and unmake themselves, in which Lewis himself, as actor, continually appears as "someone else," refusing to remain in any position.

In *The Total Film-Maker,* Lewis writes:

> A man who is going to write, produce, direct, and act in a film argues more with himself, fights a greater battle than any battle with all the other bright committee minds choosing to give him static. The battle within himself is part and parcel of what makes him a total film-maker. He struggles within one mind. One hat fights the other. Often the actor cannot stand what the director says. The producer thinks the director is a moron. And the writer is disturbed by all three of them. The total film-maker cannot lie to any of his separate parts and be successful. There is a tremendous inner government within him, and his judgment is severely examined by that inner government. (24)

Being total means being at war with oneself. In his films, Lewis finds this inner struggle in, and projects it onto, the world, which he remakes in the image of a multiplicity all of whose members (as at the end of *The Family Jewels*) demand to be recognized and coexist in a state of constant disagreement.

If the confessional aspect of *The Nutty Professor* and the self-reflexivity of films such as *The Errand Boy* and *The Patsy* have encouraged viewers to see Lewis's work as a distorted autobiography, a set of mirror fictions in which he externalizes various aspects of himself and sends them colliding against one another, his films make an equally strong demand to be read as the most vivid and emotionally wrenching American show-business hallucinations ever put on film: representations and creations of a modern world in part naturalistic and plausible, in part fantastic and implausible, partly real, partly staged. In describing them like this, I don't mean to say that they are films in which, simply, "anything goes" (though *Cracking Up* comes close to such a condition). Films such as *The Bellboy, The Errand Boy, The Nutty Professor, The Patsy, Three on a Couch,* and *The Big Mouth* are comic masterpieces that propose a rich and haunting combination of realms of seeing and experiencing, of values that denounce each other without ceasing to coexist within a single frame. These films do not, and are not made to, compel diegetic belief or offer the reassurance of a cohesive narrative controlled by a stable authorial agency. They set up, instead, a liberating and exhilarating confusion of roles and realms in which the author is one of the figures that swim in and out of focus.

Notes

1. My translation. Unless an English edition is listed in the bibliography, all translations from French are mine.
2. The version of *Hardly Working* that was released to U.S. television and home video is missing about six and a half minutes of footage (available in European versions) from the last twenty minutes of the film. The missing scenes make the progression of Bo's view of himself somewhat clearer without fully resolving the ambiguities of the film.
3. Lewis performed the same skit—about a movie fan who ingeniously crashes a black-tie-and-tails premiere—on the *Jerry Lewis Show* on December 27, 1957.
4. See *The Patsy* scripts dated December 31, 1963, and February 4, 1964, in the Paramount Pictures collection, Academy of Motion Pictures Arts and Sciences Library, Los Angeles. (See also Benayoun 179.)
5. "Order-word" seems to have become the favored English equivalent for the term *mot d'ordre,* as used by Gilles Deleuze and Félix Guattari in *Capitalisme et schizophrénie.*
6. We see this emptiness, at any rate, when the film is shown at or around the Academy ratio; cropped to a widescreen projection ratio, as it is in the Paramount DVD, the marginal space at the top and the bottom of the screen is not visible. It might be assumed that this is how Lewis and the cinematographer W. Wallace Kelley intended the film to be seen, but they were also aware that it would be shown uncropped on TV and in 16mm. Whether or not the space around the house is visible, it is clear that the shot is designed to emphasize the status of the house as a movie set.

An Interview with Jerry Lewis |

(The following interview was conducted on July 28, 29, and 30, 2003, in San Diego.)

CHRIS FUJIWARA: Could we start by talking about some of the directors you worked with early on, like Norman Taurog, George Marshall, and of course Frank Tashlin, and what you learned from them?

JERRY LEWIS: I'll tell you something interesting about Taurog. Taurog taught me some of the most important information for me to become a good director, and that was what not to do. I'm trying not to make it sound like he wasn't good. He was a good director. He knew what to do and how to get it. But the way he did it, I learned not to do it that way.

CF: What way was that?

JL: Cajole, curry favor. Deceptive. Not terribly sincere. I watched all that.

CF: What about George Marshall? That's a director that people don't talk about too much.

JL: George Marshall was very inventive. The beauty of George Marshall was his natural sense of humor, which he took to the set with him. Suffice to say that Norman had a sense of humor, but he put that in his locker. He came to conduct business. George Marshall came to play. Big difference. And the fact that he had directed Laurel and Hardy [*Pack Up Your Troubles*, "Their First Mistake," and "Towed in a Hole," all 1932] put him in a place in my eyes that was quite special. Because Stan Laurel would never have allowed him three minutes on the set unless he was qualified. In the last five years of Stan's life I spent maybe every Sunday with him. If he said George Marshall was okay, you'd better just go with him. Which I did. Though I had no choice: that was our first director [*My Friend Irma*, 1949]. I had no say in the matter. Later on I had say in the matter, and I got him whenever I could. But he was wonderfully innovative. That's the best thing I can say about George. He did what Joe Mankiewicz taught me as a director: Create an atmosphere for fun, and you'll get great work. Not fun ha-ha, but fun rather than stress. Create an atmosphere for fun.

I said, "Joe"—Mankiewicz, that is—"you created an atmosphere for fun on *All about Eve*?" He said, "Absolutely. The actors have got the material in their head. There's no reason to keep it stress-like when we're getting set or rehearsing. I don't want them to go full-out in a rehearsal, so I keep it light." And, boy, did he teach me! When you want it on film, go for it. But if you rehearse it enough, you'll get take one. The magic of what you're going to do in comedy is that you're going to want spontaneity. You don't get that in take fifteen. You get a technical, regimented, robot-like piece of material. He was right.

You know, a lot of the work of the director, which I'm sure you know, is off the cuff. And not because they're incompetent. Sometimes it's because they did not learn the most important part of the process is homework. And because they did it that way a number of times, they believed that they did it right. Well, I would like to show you some films done by directors that winged it, and what they could have been. They were wonderful the way they were. But they could have been masterpieces with homework.

CF: It's interesting what you say about Marshall being more fun and creating a better environment, because it seems to me that of the two, and it may have been a matter of the scripts to some extent, Taurog's films seem to be a little better. Taurog directed, for example, *Living It Up,* which is one of the best Martin and Lewis films, in my opinion.

JL: That was codirected.

CF: Codirected with you. I was going to ask . . .

JL: Yes.

CF: Especially the dance with Sheree North, where . . .

JL: Yeah. Definitely. And the big dance number with the hundred girls. It was really well laid out. Norman Taurog was the kind of a man that couldn't share a credit. And I wouldn't take it because of my relationship with my partner. But in talking about it in the confines of the production, he didn't have any way of doing that. So I kept my mouth shut, too. Not important. A credit among those producing the film? Not important.

CF: Could you tell me a little more about in what sense you codirected a scene like the dance in *Living It Up?*

JL: I was very technically oriented. Norman was not. Norman knew nothing about the camera, which always disturbed me. That's almost like a surgeon frightened of a scalpel. No different. And I made it my business to learn in the first year what this was about, you know. The first year that Dean and I were on the lot, they couldn't find me. I was in the camera department, I was in editing, I was in miniatures, in wardrobe, in makeup, in post; they had to find me to get me to get on the stage and do a scene. By the end of the second year I could thread a BNC camera. I could lens-change any instrument, and I could edit any kind of sound material on a Moviola, and make edits. I really learned fast. Norman, not knowing technical, he would . . . in the beginning, the first film I did with Norman, I watched him say to a cinematographer, "I want a two shot." I later learned the reason I was upset about that was because there are thirty thousand two shots. Which two shot? What kind of two shot? Straight two shot, fifty-fifty? Over-on, over-on? Single pull? Single to a deuce? Start the deuce, stay with the deuce? How many two shots does the cinematographer have to choose from? I said "No, that'll never do." When I started to direct, I sat on that camera. I made the two shot and built the marks and the moves for that two shot. And anyone that didn't do that, couldn't be taught to do that on the spot, so I would very diplomatically say, "Norman, this is a three-camera shoot. You need the whole thing, 'cause there's a hundred girls. You need the deuce of Dean and Jerry, but you better have a single on the fuckin' money. Get a single on the kid. And we got it all. The two of them, beautiful. Oh, and the single on the kid is a transport. Get him for thirty feet, get Dean for thirty feet. Transport. We'll have all we want of the singles." I told Norman about it; [he said,] "That's very good." He never argued with me about the technical. That's how it got done in many, many cases. Because to direct the people and not complement it by the technical, what was the point? You're going to direct the people to do certain things and not see it, or not be able to put it on film? So I was a stickler with that. I lived on the camera.

CF: On a film like *Living It Up,* would you invariably go through Norman Taurog with suggestions like that, or would you work directly with the cinematographer?

JL: No, no, no, no, no, no, no. You never do that. That's going over his head. Go to Norman. And very often, we had good cinematographers that would hear me, and they're doing this. [Nods.] You know, they understand completely. I'm talking their language, and behind Norman, they'd be going. . . . [Nods.] You know, "Someone's telling me what they want." The biggest thing in Hollywood is indecision. And great technicians need to be told, "What do you want? What is it that you want me to do for you?" "Give me a two shot." Well, now, he's going to make *his* two shot. Isn't there a vision in your head, how this two shot should look? It's either here, or there, over-on, way there, head to toe, what are you talking about? So it's the cinematographer's choice. When the director looks at the rushes, he knew he asked for a two shot, and he sees one, and it's fine. I battled that throughout.

CF: You did get credit on *Money from Home,* which Marshall directed, for the musical sequences, which I guess referred to the record scene under the balcony and the scene with the animals. Was that the same kind of situation, where you talked to Marshall about how you thought it should be done?

JL: He asked me if I had any ideas of how to deal with that. And I went to Dean and said, "You know, this is something that'll work, and I'm gonna write the music for it." "No problem." That was it. I never did a film with any of those directors, even at the beginning, where I wasn't codirecting with them. On a very quiet, silent, behind-the-scenes level, because I couldn't take the chance of alienating my partner.

CF: Did you also codirect with Tashlin?

JL: Everything. Everything Tashlin did with me, we did together. Right from the first one, right to *Hollywood or Bust*. We did it together. He was my teacher. But when he was leaving Paramount and he decided to retire, he wrote me a farewell letter; the salutation was, "Dear Teacher." Which was pretty nice.

CF: What specifically did you learn from him?

JL: I learned the world of cartoon. I learned that we could take a great cartoon that's dead in the water, what we call dead in the water, boatmen, a cartoon that's dead on the paper, no animation, it's a cartoon, there is a caption, and that's it. Frank believed we could make the cartoon live. And not use a caption but fun dialogue. He taught me that. He also taught me to look at the people that I'm staging and put them in the cartoon form in my mind and see how it looks. It was very interesting.

CF: Can you think of an example where the cartoon form is there with the live person?

JL: In *Cinderfella*, a scene with Dame Judith Anderson, Robert Hutton, Henry Silva, and myself. It was critical to the story, so much information, it was a very important exposition scene. You know the term "exposition"? That's very rarely considered sometimes in a movie. Frank and I were very strong about it, doing it all in this. So in staging it, I went nowhere near it. I just was one of the actors, as Frank was staging it with eleven moves of the camera. Eleven. Four people: nasty stepbrother, nasty stepbrother, the kid, stepmother. Eleven moves. The brother in a single, the brother in a double, the single-double, track-pan of mother, mother crosses to brothers, mother crosses to the kid, mother crosses down, comes back to original mark, brothers cross to mother, both go up to. . . . Frank said, "I see the cartoon pages." [He makes a clicking sound.] He saw this flipping. We used to call them O. Henry books. We would hold them up to the light, the broads. Tillie Toiler was one of them. Another one was Harold Teen. The first picture's got a rail on this long, and a broad is coming to sit on it, but you'd have to turn the pages to see all this dirty stuff.[1] And Frank sees the movement of the mother to the sons, up to the kid, back to her place, the sons going, hitting her, coming up, conferring, going back: he saw all this in individual cartoons, and he put it together, and goddamn if the scene didn't work that way. It was supposed to be stoic [*sic*], and it was. We were kind of riveted in the material, 'cause it was heated, and he wanted . . . and he did it. It was brilliant. But he first saw it here flipping, and that's how he staged it. It was great.

CF: Is it possible to separate in a film like *Cinderfella* or *The Disorderly Orderly* what came from Tashlin and what came from you, or was it too much together?

JL: It was way too much together. I mean, Frank wouldn't walk on the set until he knew I was on the lot. It became as close as Siamese, we were with the projects. *Rock-a-Bye [Baby]*, we had such a love affair with that movie, because he had just become a grandfather, so the babies meant so much to him. My being a new father at the time meant so much. So we never left one another's side on that movie. We really worked together.

CF: In *Cinderfella*, there are things that remind me so much of you and less of him, like the famous stairway scene, and the Basie orchestra coming out, that's something that could be right out of one of your movies . . .

JL: Yeah. I could tell you. . . . In *Cinderfella*, I could tell you the portions. It's unethical to diminish the other writer, as it were, but Frank was the first to tell everybody that the whole ball I wrote from scratch. I wrote the ball from the very first shot of the ball, their presence, what was happening, the delivery of the Basie orchestra on the lazy Susan, the kid's entrance, the movement, the scene, the dance. It was my baby. And Frank knew what I had on the paper and didn't know about what the stairs were going to be. Because it was one take. And I knew what I choreographed in my head to that music. I didn't even rehearse it for camera. I made camera setups with Frank. I said, "You're gonna need this, you're gonna really need this, this move is vital." So we're up on the crane for his entrance, and I needed the crane to move with him. I didn't want to tilt or pan with him, I wanted to boom with him, to keep his head and his toes in the shot, right down to here, till he does that wild walk in front of the people. So once I had the camera set, and Frank yelled, "You're ready?" I said, "Let's go." Hit the playback, and down I came, and he stood by the side of the camera, and I saw, during what I was doing, I saw—just joy in his . . . he couldn't believe what I was doing. Chris, what I was doing was part of my body language, that's all. I put music to it. But yet women saw that. The mail we got on the sexual connotation—What sex? That crazy bastard walking down the stairs? Yeah, we got a lot of that.

CF: One film that you and Tashlin did, *Who's Minding the Store?*, I read in an interview with you that that was Tashlin's baby.

JL: Yes, it's true. It was. He had a wonderful time with that. And I couldn't contribute any more than the actor. It was his baby, so I left it to him. Pretty much the same story with *Disorderly Orderly*. That was another of his babies: I laid back and just took direction. It was wonderful. Well, he was getting to know me pretty well, so he was writing for me.

CF: Moving on to the films you directed, there are moments in most of them when one of the characters speaks directly to the audience, such as the narrator at the end of *The Bellboy*, or in *The Ladies Man*, when the sympathetic girl says that nice people are always needed, or in *The Errand Boy*, the scene with the puppets, which nobody else would do.

JL: We call that a director with steel balls. I just loved what it did. The stuff that I do that's really good is when I have the right intention. It's not necessarily the material as much as it is the intention and the material. When my intention was to make it soft and sensitive and loving, that's what I got out of it. Whether it belonged in the movie or not. You'll get your naysayers to say, "What was that for?" What was it for when Chaplin sat at the edge of the street and just watched people walking by? I mean, what did that mean? It meant something: it meant he wasn't going anywhere. I don't think that you can be so analytical that you knock good ideas out of your brain. I loved doing the puppets. I don't know why, but I did. You're not the first to mention it, either.

CF: That's a beautiful scene. It's a little out of tone with the rest of the movie, but quite deliberately so.

JL: Absolutely.

CF: You handle it in a very realistic way. It's almost more realistic than the rest of the movie.

JL: I shot it like I did two people in a scene.

CF: In many scenes in your films you speak directly to the audience, like when Kelp on stage near the end of *The Nutty Professor* says, "You'd better like yourself," or the end of *The Bellboy*, "You never know the other guy's story unless you ask," or in *The Patsy* when Ina Balin talks about how the bad things that happen to us make us better people. I have a feeling that you put these statements in there because these are things that you believe and you want to use the film to express them directly to the people watching. Is that true?

JL: If you can be an influence on young people with something that's meaningful, I believe in it. Sometimes I have been accused of being morally theatrical. I hate that. I'm moral. Whether it's theatrical or I'm walking with my dog. I like to think I'm moral. There's a wonderful line: "I care about the demise of a man because I'm involved with mankind." My involvement is genuine, it's sincere. I feel that if you're given a special place in this life, you can't walk into a small room and close the door with it. I think that's wrong. Because it'll be of no consequence to yourself or anyone else, unless you use that gift. Use it how? To get another gift? No, you use that gift to spread the word that made you the recipient of the gift. So I'm kind of idealistic, mid-Victorian, completely old-fashioned. I can't help that. That's the way I am, that's the way I think.

I think that for years we have recognized the author by what he writes. An author will always—you will do the same, Chris—a writer tips his mitt. If a writer would like to be completely anonymous about the character and fabric of the man, don't write, 'cause you can't hide in writing. I just believe it. I'm sure there are people who will tell me that I'm crazy—"Oh, well, what about J. D. Salinger?" That was J. D. Salinger. J. D. Salinger was Holden Caulfield. Don't tell me that was a fictitious character out of the mind of his deep deep deep imagination. Bullshit. He was Holden Caulfield.

So, what my writings were, in my conscious mind, were: I needed to balance the comedy. I always got to the point where I needed to settle the audience. And more importantly, to see that he [Lewis's character] is of some consequence and not a fool. If they see him of some consequence, everything he does will be that much funnier, and everything he does will be that much more real, and the foolish and silly and mischief, and all of those things that come down the pike in a film, will be accepted as valid because of that exposition early on. You can wait till almost the middle of the movie to do it. To protect that last four reels or five reels.

CF: Like you do in *The Errand Boy.*

JL: Yeah. I was very conscious of those moments because Chaplin did it from beginning to end. It rode alongside of his genius. The common man and Chaplin. Chaplin being beneath the common man. The Tramp. Chaplin could never have driven a message across to the public without the Tramp. Proof: Chaplin got in trouble when he pressed his pants. My own opinion. When I said it to Charlie, he said, "I've heard it a couple of different ways, Jerry. But that's as succinct and as on-the-mark as I've ever heard." I was talking about *Monsieur Verdoux*. I said, "Charlie, you couldn't be Tramp-like with pressed pants. You knew that, and I know it. But I loved *Monsieur Verdoux*. I loved that character who didn't have a chance. You put this character on top of thirty-two years of the Tramp. Come on, you can't do that and expect it to fly immediately. Same with *Limelight*." He said, "But I had to break out. I needed to do those things for my own creative juices." I said, "Charlie, I'm not damning you. What you did, I would have done in a minute. You stretched." The very thing that a good comic director must do is stretch.

CF: Is that related to what you meant when you wrote that nothing is more dramatic than comedy?

JL: That statement comes from doing comedy. In order to make your audience laugh, you have to dramatically change who you are. I won't trip over that piece of wood on the stage if it's me walking there. But Jerry will, or Stanley, or the Idiot, or whatever we call him in that moment. He *has* to trip over it. Now, he has to turn into something that isn't truly him, so we're taking a piece of vanity and rubbing it out, a little ego, burying it, sandpapering all that down, and bringing up all of the gargoyles. Because in England they say what he does is grotesque. The first time I read that, I was heartbroken, but they say, "No, that's a compliment." Okay. When I stand in front of an audience on New Year's Eve, let's say, years ago, and I see the young man and his girl, man and his wife, girl, boyfriend, couples, lovers, all that wonderful stuff ringside. I'm standing up there alone and making a fucking fool of myself to entertain all of them. There's nothing more dramatic than that moment, Chris. It's very dramatic. Because I have to call on something that's not what I want to be at that moment. I want to be there with my girl or my wife watching some other schmuck make a fool of himself. But I never ever thought of what I did as demeaning. What I thought of it was: other than me at that moment. So it's very dramatic.

I love when somebody said, "Did you ever think of doing drama?" What? Do you really think that Jack Nicholson does drama? He reads material, he's directed in the scene, and he plays it as a very good actor. There's nothing dramatic about that. He's a very good actor reading the words and not bumping into the furniture. When you ask a comedian if he ever would do anything dramatic—he's done it from the day he decided to make people laugh! He's far more dramatic than any dramatic actor. Sir Laurence Olivier said to me, "I wish I knew your drama." He knew what I was talking about. Red Skelton would have given his soul to walk out on the stage accepted as George C. Scott was. Uh-uh, it's not in the cards. That's not what they pay you for. Get back behind the clown, mister. Very dramatic. You don't have to ask Sir Gielgud to be dramatic; you ask him to act and learn the words and do the scene. Of course it's called a drama because it's a story of a man who lost his son, and it's terrible. But it's not as dramatic as this.

CF: That's an extraordinary definition. I never understood that before. Does that relate to why in so many of your films you play against yourself? In *The Bellboy,* you're both Stanley and Jerry Lewis. In *The Nutty Professor,* you're the two people. Is that the drama in the comedy, the conflict between . . .

JL: You have to have—the word is magic: conflict. You know, without conflict, you have nothing. Because without conflict, you can't have a rooting interest. And the thing that defines great comedy is when you get an audience to root for the comic. Not just watch him fly by a scene but hope he's okay. My children watching a Jerry Lewis movie would ask, "Is Daddy okay?" if it ever looked like I was in harm's way. My daughter does the same thing, "Is Daddy okay?" But then she'll ask her mother, "May I see a Jerry Lewis movie?"

CF: You said you put in moments, like in *The Errand Boy* and *The Patsy,* where we feel what's serious, what the stakes are for this character, why it's important to watch him apart from his being funny. Are there moments like that in *The Ladies Man?*

JL: Where there's heart out there? His love scene with Pat Stanley, trying desperately to be that young man that might be her choice possibly. His eagerness to please is a very very marvelous attribute in the life of a comic because audiences can relate to that. Most everybody means to please. That's why we fear rejection so desperately, because we're trying so hard. But again, I write what I can at that one specific time for the audience to recognize there's substance. You cannot have an audience believe there's substance going off the back end of a car into a pool. It's far from substantial in the mind's eye of the individual watching. But moments like I try to provide are substantial. The equation and the dynamic isn't so that they recognize he's very bright; it's got nothing to do with intelligence. It has to do with his sensitivity as a human being, and they can identify with that. And they root for him because of that. And once you've got them rooting for you, you got it made. Then you can do anything. You can do unfunny things that they will enjoy because they already have committed to rooting for you, you know. So it's almost a wonderful skeleton key to a lock you can open all the time. You're doing a great physical bit, and you've done so much in the film, and when I get a huge physical sequence that I'm going to do, that I know is very important, stuff before that has to be meaningful, before I go to that big physicality.

The singing teacher in *The Patsy,* for example. I mean, I worked months on catching those vases. I'll tell you exactly, it was five weeks that I worked on it, before I would shoot it. Because I had to get the weights and measures perfectly. . . . It was such an important scene, 'cause he was alone on the screen, and he was. . . . The secret of what I always did, was a man in trouble. That's what comedy is: a man in trouble. To watch him with those vases, it was—I mean, people in theaters applauded it, which made me feel very good about it. I needed substance in him before that, so it wouldn't look like just Three Stooges. 'Cause I hated for any slapstick that I did to look like I just did it. I liked that it might have taken a long time to prepare.

CF: You're not afraid to go a long time with the scene, too. It's a very extended scene.

JL: You bet. I'm not afraid of that, because I also believe that once we got the laughter in it, and if you can go further in the scene to maintain what you did earlier in making him substantial, you do that. Most comic directors will go for the joke and cut. I like the tail-off of getting him back into the norm, as it were. A lot of that was by design, but I have to tell you, Chris, a lot of it was lucky. I did a lot of stuff on the set that I would turn to people and say, "I didn't want to do that. It worked great! Let's do that. Why did I do that?" My first assistant said to me one day, "Why the hell do you care why? You did." I said, "It's important. I may want to do it again sometime." He said, "You'll never do it again sometime. But what you do the next time will be because you thought something differently." And he was right.

CF: You mentioned Pat Stanley in *The Ladies Man*. I like her performance in that film, and I like how low-key the scenes between you and her are. They're not played for laughs.

JL: No, never. Never for laughs. She was the umbilical between him and real for a while.

CF: And it seems to me that Ina Balin in *The Patsy* has a similar function.

JL: Yeah. Because there was such hysteria in the seven roles. I tried so much quick movement, specifically to keep him cocoonlike among them. And she was cool and smooth against all of their animation. Remember I had Everett Sloane, Peter Lorre, John Carradine, Phil Harris, Keenan Wynn—all five, directors in summer stock, in plays, in films, and so on. I've got five directors that I'm working with, all of whom watched very closely and had infinite respect for the director. It was wonderful. But to get fire under their ass was almost impossible. I finally had to confer with them. "Let me tell you what you have to do to help me make him work." Then it started to work. But I always kept Ina—"Remember that in his eyes you're a wonderful-looking chick he'd love to ball, and in your eyes, he's a wonderful kid you'd like to help." Big difference in those two bottoms of the people. She saw tremendous value in him as the film went on. She saw things he did that had value, that he was not just this bellman they put together and said, "Let's make a star." Third quarter of the film, she started to see him being fairly practical, reasonable, for the lack of a better word: normal. Otherwise it would never have connected.

CF: You use character actors like Helen Traubel, Iris Adrian, Howard McNear, Neil Hamilton . . .

JL: Great, great actors. Neil Hamilton, he had probably the most experience of any actor in Hollywood.

CF: You encourage these people to do a very stylized acting, almost over-the-top.

JL: Absolutely. There's no way in the world that you can have them play type. You've got to recognize who they're in the scene with. And who's coming up after them. And what they must be substantially before he comes. So in asking them to broaden their performance, and that—

trust me that I will smooth it, I won't let it go to that place that [creates] discomfort for an actor, knowing they're over the top—I'll take it to a point between where you're fine, midway to over the top is fine for me. But I need it all. Let me take it to that wonderful resolve that I know I can use for the reason that I'm doing it. Once you explain it to them, I mean, it's wonderful.

CF: You didn't have resistance from them?

JL: A couple of times I'd get resistance from an actress like Katie [Kathleen Freeman]. Katie was afraid that I was teaching her the acting process. She never ever said it, but she gave me all kinds of static, and I finally said to her—as a matter of fact, I think it was on *The Ladies Man*, when I said, "Katie, I'm not trying to teach you anything. I'm really trying to stylize you for what we're doing here." And she heard the word, and she locked in in a second. But I said, "I'm not satisfied that I have verbally made you understand. I want you to do something for me now. Let me print it, and let me do it a second way, and show you what I mean." So I did an improvisation with her. I shot it. And then I said, "Now, let's do it exactly as written." Which we did. And I ran it for her. And she went, "Oh." I said, "Is that all?" She said, "That's all you're gonna get. But: Oh." She saw it. Which I did with actors all the time. I never showed them the good they did. I only showed them the wrong they did. And immediately they're seeing it. Words never did it. Words weren't clear. Because they immediately became, "Whose fault is this?" "Wait. I'm not reprimanding you. I'm saying it's not what I want, because you're bringing it something I don't need. And I can't tell you what that is. So let me show it to you. Come." And I'd run it. And they'd go, "Oh, yeah." I said, "Let's drop that." Do it again: on the fuckin' money. Perfect.

CF: Was there ever an actor that you had to end up accepting a compromise because you couldn't get them to do what you had in mind for the part?

JL: [Pause.] I thought there was one. He just needed more spoon-feeding than most. Terrific actor. But not under my tutelage. He was a terrific actor in things I've seen him do. As a matter of fact, I grew up with him. It was Edward Arnold. Remember the name? Had that great laugh when he did Diamond Jim Brady. I thought I would lose him. But my patience with an actor served me well. That was a movie,

Living It Up, where I split the directorial chores. And I worked closely with Edward. Only time.

CF: Did you ever give a line reading?

JL: You never give actors line readings. You say to them, "The line reading you're giving it is pretty shitty. Would you like to give me a couple more?"

CF: There are moments in your films when I think I see the actors imitating you.

JL: I watched that very closely. I didn't want that to happen. If it got through, I missed it. Actors will pick up your rhythm. Other than that, no, I wouldn't allow it. If I saw it, I'd dump it. Or if I saw it and it was effective, and didn't appear to be what you thought it was, then I'd keep it. But I had a tremendous . . . directorially, I had a fearless courage. Which helped me tremendously.

CF: How would the fearlessness work with your work with actors?

JL: I was fearless in that I would dig deep in myself for them to see that they can go a little way too. I never ever allowed them to think they were wrong. I'd always cut—"Goddamn fan!" I would yell, "Goddamn fan is on, anybody know that?" Nobody's looking. There was no fan. While we stopped, I'd say to the actor, "By the way, do such-and-such here, it'll be better." Then I'll go the other actor that I had nothing for, and I'd say, "That thing we talked about is perfect. Let's go." So there's no one ever attacked in any way. If it got bad, I'd move a scene to another time. Take the actor to lunch. I'd either fix it or recast it. That's what I mean about plutonium balls. 'Cause a director never took a chance of having to reshoot something out of fear. Fear, my ass. I had brought in, on *The Bellboy,* [an actress whom] I warned that her conduct was unacceptable. Snapping her fingers at members of my crew. I said, "Unacceptable, kid. Now please don't do it." Two days went by, it was okay. Three days. Now the fourth day—[snaps fingers]. I called my production manager and said, "Get her off the set, get her clothes and send her back to Hollywood." He said, "You've shot four days with her." I said, "Who asked you for a fucking rundown? Do what I tell you." Done. I jumped the board, went ahead with other scenes, called L.A., got a gal I knew would be fine, flew her down, I reshot four days, so fucking what? But it was fun, and she was better. Everyone loved her, I loved her, I got good material. Everything benefited by that move.

Had I kept the other one, it would have been expeditious and that's all. Sorry, not my movie. You know, I figure that the four days that cost at that time a hundred thousand dollars, a lot of money for the budget that I had, I was protecting a million. I think 10 percent insurance is worth it; that's what I think. But that's unheard of.

CF: You must have been one of the only directors in Hollywood at that time who'd make a deliberate effort to cast very oldtime character actors like Mike Mazurki, Vince Barnett, Benny Rubin, Jay Adler. . . . These were people that you didn't see in a lot of theatrical films at the time.

JL: Good actors. Nothing better than an experienced actor. And you're never going to get the experience with an actor that's new. I felt so comfortable working with actors that I respected from what I'd seen them do in the past. It was a wonderful feeling for me to have the pleasure to direct them. They gave me more, I cannot tell you. You embrace them and give them love, they'll go through walls for you. Any actor. If they see hostility or temperament, or disdain, you lose them. They're gone! And you can't get 'em back with a present. They're the same as a puppy whose spirit you've broken. Case closed. I know no better analogy.

CF: In *The Ladies Man*, both in the scene with the hat and Buddy Lester, and the scene with George Raft, you start with a situation that's basically realistic, and then it turns into something completely different.

JL: The black hat was written minimally just to introduce the date for one of the girls. It was one of those things that I had written very sparsely to include an outside character to the house. When we got into it, there was sheer hysteria on the set. I couldn't contain the crew, I couldn't contain me, and Buddy broke every fifteen seconds. There was nothing we could do about it. It was one of those wonderful giggle days. That I got the material I got was a miracle, 'cause had I called everyone back tomorrow, it would have changed everything. It was one of those wonderful giggles, and I think I was responsible for most of it because I have such an affinity with the actor. It isn't that often that someone else makes me laugh. When that happens, it's glorious. Plus I was rooting so hard for Buddy to be good in it. 'Cause that kind of a credit is important to a comic. So between rooting and giggling and nurturing the scene because I cared so much about it, it developed into quite a scene. Ultimately it wound up being what I think is a classic comedy scene, with the comic giving it all over to the other comedian. Which I love doing anyhow, simply 'cause I learned that from Jack Benny. Jack had two lines on one radio program. I said, "You were practically not in the show, Jack." He said, "I was practically not in the *Jack Benny* program." Which is a wonderful philosophy. "Whether I was there or not, they're going to talk about the *Jack Benny* program." So I've given it all to them and let them have their moment. I learned a great deal from my dad about generosity and giving to the other actors, because it propels you into a place that you would not normally be in had you not decided to be generous and selfless.

CF: The whole scene depends on Buddy Lester's reaction. What makes the scene work is that sudden change—he starts out being menacing and tough, then he completely collapses. Which is totally unexpected and wild. Did you conceive of that when you were writing it, or did it happen when you were rehearsing and shooting it?

JL: I think it happened. As I say, I wrote an absolutely strategic scene without any real hope that it would go any further than that, a pat scene, for the reason I expounded on before. But a scene will very often take you to a place you didn't figure on, and then you get all kinds of credit for creating this wonderful thing. I find it difficult to understand an awful lot of the stuff that happens, which I think is part of the creative process. I'm sure that you know what I'm talking about. How many times have you written something that you thought was—not so much inane, but minimal, and someone else would look at it and think it was just spectacular? "What the hell are you talking about? That?" Well, you didn't plan for it to be that way. You were hoping to get through it, because you were staggering through a moment in time that wasn't really that productive for you, but you wound up finding it was better than anything else you had done, and that's incredible when that happens.

CF: The scene with George Raft in *The Ladies Man* is similar in that everything depends on the change in Raft's attitude toward you. He suddenly becomes obsessed with the need to prove to you that he's George Raft.

JL: In writing *The Ladies Man,* I had gone to a dinner party with some mutual friends of Raft's, and I come to find out that he's struggling and having a tough time. And that breaks my heart when I hear that. So I decided to write a scene so that I could pay him. He was very proud; he wouldn't take any handouts. Same thing with Stan Laurel. Very proud, as I'd like to think I would be in those circumstances. So I really wrote what I thought would be a funny scene, while at the same time showing the extent of the kid's imagination. I always like to think that that whole dance sequence was in his mind. Whether that came across to the customer or not, I don't know. It just worked the way it was. Of course, young people today that look at it don't know what it means. They don't know George Raft and that he was in *Bolero,* or that he was considered one of the best dancers in Hollywood. But it worked. I loved it, it looked so rich and so movie-like [see fig. 16].

CF: I wanted to talk to you about the "movie" look of your films. That seems to have been very conscious with you from the beginning. Even *The Bellboy,* which is not a studio film, has . . .

JL: A lot of that. Almost taking people past the fourth wall. I love knocking down the fourth wall, all the time.

CF: Which you do to great effect in *The Ladies Man,* when you pull the camera back so we see the doll's house and the empty space in front of it, and you do that in the Raft scene too, with the spotlight and the empty space.

JL: I sit on the camera, and I block the shot. I have to see what I want to see in the end result. In structuring a scene, I always kept fore-

Figure 16. "So rich and so movie-like": Jerry Lewis and George Raft in *The Ladies Man.*

ground very important. Every aspect of the frame was important to me: I filled it, and marked it, and watched it, whereas a lot of directors will look at the focal point, the artist, the actor, the actress, the prop, dead center of the frame. If it's a joke, it better be there. If it's exposition, if you're building, if you're moving into a situation that you want clear to the audience, you gotta do it all, you just have to do it all. I didn't learn that from anyone; it was instinctive with me right from the beginning. If you're going to point the camera, point it at what you want the people to see. Don't hide anything, unless it shouldn't be seen.

CF: What was important to you about what this "movie" look? Why is that such a big element in your films?

JL: Because as a child, I was enthralled with thinking about who was watching. Spencer Tracy in *Captains Courageous.* Remember the film? Who was over here? Who was their fourth wall? The sea, the ship, Tracy in the water dying. It's not real. He is not dying, he's not going to die. So there's people here watching this. God, would I love to be there with them. To watch it. I would have wanted to see it as I saw it first, and then, could I see it the other way? It was always my desire to peek behind the scenes. I was always behind-the-scenes-conscious and knew that moments of behind-the-scenes for an audience just uplifted them. Whether they thought about it or not, if you show it to them, they're going to see it. They're either going to like it or not understand it. Most people love it. Or maybe in the back of my mind I always felt it would be good to never take them so deeply that they forget it's a movie. I think David Lean needed to do that, so that you'd forget it was a movie. [Fred] Zinnemann would do that. Great directors I think did it most of the time. They're careful not to make the audience conscious that it's a movie. Frank Tashlin had a fetish about green. Shrubbery placed in the scene by a shrubbery man. He hated it, he never could get the pure color of a grass lawn or bushes. So I said, "Frank, take it out of the studio, get what you want." We would do that sometime, just because he needed to see that. He was obsessed with the ugly color of studio-prop green.

CF: Why did you want to remind the audience that it's a movie?

JL: Well, I don't know that I wanted to shake them up, "Hey, this is a movie!" But I was hoping there were kids out there that would feel about it as I did. That's all that was. I never wanted it to be so far and away from reality that your audience would look at it as a distant faction.

Whereas I had to do that in *Cinderfella:* I had to keep the audience over there as a distant faction.

CF: Because of the fantasy quality of it?

JL: Yeah. I couldn't let Ed Wynn come in as the Fairy Godfather. I couldn't let him come downstage too much. I kept everything at a place where I thought was much more advantageous to the total film.

CF: Your movies are all very lavish. There's so much emphasis on the hugeness of the sets, not just *The Ladies Man,* but even in *The Family Jewels,* where you start in the lawyer's office and you end in the room where she makes her decision. Those are huge sets, with beautiful floors and walls and colors. This seems to have been really important to you, to get a look of expensiveness and luxury into these films.

JL: That's what Hollywood glamour was supposed to be about. You don't think films would have been successful if they were all about the apartment that a man and woman live in, in New York, a cold-water flat? If everything was like that, we wouldn't have films. We have films today because of *42nd Street, Broadway Rhythm, An American in Paris.* Lavish was part of Hollywood's glamour. You could buy a ticket to go to a movie to see things you would not see in your real life. If you had a respect for your audience to that degree, you would concentrate on it, and I did. Plus I wanted to take pride in what I was doing. So if you look at the sets in *Three on a Couch,* it uplifts an audience with great color.

CF: In *Three on a Couch,* especially the set of Chris's apartment, there's so much emphasis on those colors, they really pop off the screen.

JL: Well, he was an artist, and I felt he'd live that way. He was contemporary, kind of progressive, upscale, why put him in an apartment that was down?

CF: Keeping that lavishness, that Hollywood glamour in that period in your films strikes me as almost a radical gesture because of what was happening in Hollywood at that time. I think of your films as almost the last survival of this Hollywood glamour. Even during the sixties, everything had already changed, as you know better than I. Is it possible to look at *The Errand Boy* as a film that comments on the changes in Hollywood?

JL: Not in my conscious mind, no. I just played games with the system to a degree. One of the best lines in the whole film was, "Yeah, but the hours are lousy." That was Bill's creation, Bill Richmond. He came up with that line. I said, "Shit, that's funny." I don't know that I was really very conscious . . . I was very conscious of doing a specific thing with my work that I have to admit to you had been received by people like you on a much higher level than I had anticipated. In other words, the work that I was doing I thought was as good as I could do, but I never ever put it in a place where I thought I'd get eight best-director-of-the-year awards around the world. I mean, the first one shook me, and I got shook every time I got one. It was really incredible. "Wait a minute, maybe what I'm doing ain't that bad."

CF: I love the scene in *The Family Jewels* where you put on the record "This Diamond Ring," and the scene fades. That is in the same kind of mood as the scenes with Pat Stanley in *The Ladies Man*, because suddenly the film totally switches gears, and it's just one man listening to this record and having a reaction to it. A very personal thing.

JL: Sharing a good feeling with your audience is not always bad. I don't know that they all recognized what you saw in it. That's the beauty of doing the kind of work you do where so much it is daring, risk-taking.

CF: Seeing that film as a kid, that scene always struck me in that film, not realizing it was a personal statement by you as the father of the person who did the song. So that to me is an example of the scene communicating beyond . . .

JL: What you optically see.

CF: Because of the mood of it, how quiet and real it is suddenly.

JL: The design that I would have is never just that one recording and him playing it and so on. But I'm coming from something to that, and from that going to something. So I always did everything as an arc. I never did this without hanging here and groping there. Any good director that has any quality or any competency at all does not work on the one setup. He's coming from where he was and groping to where he's going, in order for that to work right. Then there are directors who do specifically that, nothing else, next, nothing else, next, . . . I don't understand how that works, but they do it. They get it done; the movie's made, you know. Whether it's perfect, wonderful, or otherwise, I don't know. But it annoys me to think that it doesn't take that much more to do it right.

See, not enough directors recognize that when you say "roll 'em," *this* happens. [He makes an aperture shape by unclenching his fist.] That's the lens doing this. And what it's doing when you say "roll 'em," you're opening the eyes of the children in China, Russia, South America, every time you say "roll 'em," you're opening the eyes of a billion people around the world. Are we being mid-Victorian again? I don't give a shit what you call it, that's what you're doing. It was always meaningful to me. The joy of "roll 'em." But then whatever comes into it, I am there to guide it. I am either going to let it be there, or I kill it. The word "print" is very, very important to me. I don't even want to print doubt. To have it on the negative anywhere. When I'm in doubt, I'll print something. If I dislike it enough, I'll burn it, you know, just get rid of it. But I have almost a religious experience when I say "roll 'em." If a lot of young directors would know that or think of that, it would help them. I don't think it would change their ability, but it would certainly help them look at it more closely. I wonder how many directors understand that.

CF: Are there any directors that you sense in their films must have known that?

JL: David Lean. Blake Edwards. Fred Zinnemann. Joe Mankiewicz, without question. Billy Wilder. Willie Wyler. That's a pretty good list. They knew that. I don't know they did, but I would bet they did. And interestingly, Mel Brooks. He knows that, he knew that. He was very good because of that.

CF: It's interesting that you put such emphasis on this, opening the eyes, because that's an image that happens in your films. I'm thinking of how often we see somebody putting their hand right up to the camera lens, like at the end of *The Nutty Professor,* when he's taking his bow, or in *The Family Jewels,* when the photographer uncle is setting up a mount in front of the lens. That reminds me of your doing that [with the fist]: you're controlling seeing and then not seeing and then seeing again. It's very violent.

JL: Yeah. When you think of a violent director, Peckinpah. He did that all the time. Sam was a brilliant director. Though what he did was not my cup of tea. Kubrick was very involved with that. So we have a very good list. I didn't particularly care about the things that Kubrick did after *Strangelove.* I didn't need to see anything he did after that.

The director's dream is to do one work in his lifetime, in his career, and if you are lucky enough to be a director that does that one wonderful work, you've done it, that's your career.

CF: You approach sound in a very direct, materialist way, where you let the audience see and hear what's being done, and it's almost as if you were showing people how the movie is made. In *The Bellboy,* when he goes through the models' room carrying bundles of things, and he realizes they're in their underwear and puts his hand in front of the lens, at the same moment, you cut the sound.

JL: My theory is always, What you don't hear, you don't see. And I don't believe in dialogue coming over the outgoing cut, to deliver the incoming cut. I hate that. A man and a woman driving in an open convertible, and they're not talking, but you hear the argument of the two children over that cut before you go to the scene in their bedroom. What is that shit? I've always hated that, 'cause it always felt to me like, What are you, being chic?

The other thing, I was into dubbing more than any other director on the lot. Most directors would dub their film in a couple of weeks. I ran sometimes six weeks. Because I'd let them know that sound was equal to picture, and I didn't have anything with one of them gone. Am I going to release this soundtrack without images? Well, I'm not going to release the images without sound. I was a stickler on getting everything exactly the way I thought it should be. I believe you have to have both.

I've never looped a scene in a movie, ever. Take actors out on the desert, sound is bad, shoot the scene, go into dubbing, and mouth, and put voices into the mouthing. Not me. My sound man'd yell, "We can loop that, Jer!" I said, "Don't ever use that word on my set, kid, ever again. We can't loop anything. If I don't get it here on this location, it ain't gonna be in the movie, so let's adjust." I was one of the first in films to put lavaliers on. The wind for booms was terrible. I said, "Get me two lavaliers, okay? The bodies are gonna block out the wind." And damn it if I didn't make the scenes that way.

CF: There are so many great sound things in your films. In *The Ladies Man,* when they're doing the TV show, Herbert inadvertently disconnects the microphone, and you don't hear anything, which is shocking in a sound movie. I can't think of another film where in the middle of the scene suddenly there's no sound. It's experimenting with the medium in a way that's pretty daring.

JL: I didn't think of it as anything other than, that's the practical application of the joke. If you take the mic away, nobody hears anything. So I just included the audience into that scene. That's really going through the fourth wall. I had people, department heads, questioning, "Will the audience understand that when you break the cable of the mic in *Ladies Man,* are they going to understand why there's no sound?" I said, "What are you talking about? You see what he does, and you hear what happens when he does it." "Oh." But then when an audience saw it and they all approved, I would say to them, "Well, what happened with that, fellas?" "Oh, it was good, yeah." Critique in committee was always my favorite thing.

CF: Talk about breaking the fourth wall: *The Errand Boy* is a compendium of scenes that do that. One of the big examples is the dubbing of the song "Lover." What struck me about the scene in the sound studio is how beautiful and glamorous you make the singer. It struck me as this gesture of love to somebody who is an artist: in the middle of this fakery and non-art, there is art.

JL: I had no other intention than utilizing that as an important plot point of that whole sequence.

CF: Then with the payoff joke when the movie is screened and you're singing it, you draw attention to the fact that not only this was dubbed, but it can be dubbed in this funny way, too.

JL: Something I always thought about every time I was on a dubbing stage, I thought about that. I finally wrote it.

CF: You also like to associate a loud sound with a small source, like Baby in *The Ladies Man.*

JL: Yeah, with a pretty good bark.

CF: Or the small transistor radios . . .

JL: And you hear this symphony. That's just my comic sense of . . . I had written a joke that I wasn't ever able to shoot. I wouldn't even digitalize it 'cause it's too good a joke, but the joke was, "Can you turn off your pager?" Guy's going to see the Rose Bowl game on New Year's Day. "You mind turning off your pager?" "Oh, no, not at all." And he doesn't. Goes into the stadium, and they're introducing the teams, and you hear a pager. Then a pager. And then forty-five thousand pagers. Drives the two teams off the fucking field. There's no game. It's a fun joke in my head. But there's a case of visual and sound, vital.

CF: There's a lot of work with verbal humor in your films. Your double-talk scenes, like the TV repairman in *It's Only Money:* there are any number of scenes like that. It seems to me it must be impossible to script that out.

JL: The only time you see my gibberish written is when the legal department comes to me after the film and shows me what they've done phonetically. "Beldondake Bumpman." They ask, "Is Beldondake Bumpman another language?" "No." "Does it have any meaning?" "No." "Could it be another language?" "Possibly." They won't release the movie until all of this is confirmed. A legal guy with a shirt and tie comes with three assistants. "Mr. Lewis, can I ask you a couple of questions?" "Sure." "What is Banet-yech-gi-babap?" "That was a small town in Romania that I went to some years ago." "Really?" "No, I'm kidding." Every film they come to me with verifications. God almighty.

CF: A good example of that is in *Three on a Couch,* where your Rutherford character is talking about his understanding of Coleoptera.

JL: Editors went nuts. I can't write that. I'll show you the script, with "Coleoptera bit."

CF: Is that how you note it in the script?

JL: Knowing I'm going to take it somewhere. Or I'll write what I would call transient dialogue. Giving me the . . . that's where I go. I used to have wonderful people on the lot crazy. "What's he doing?" Now they see the receipts of the movie, or how well it's been received, and they don't understand. I brought Paramount eight hundred million in rentals. A lot of money. That's world, of course.

CF: You also have, in your films, a dialogue going on at the same time as your monologue, and you can see everybody on the screen, like at the prom in *The Nutty Professor:* you have Kelp doing a monologue while Del Moore and Kathleen Freeman are talking.

JL: Counterpoint.

CF: There's a moment like that in *The Ladies Man,* too, where Kathleen Freeman is talking to you about what a good job you're doing, and you repeat to yourself the instructions you've just received from Buddy Lester.

JL: Counterpoint. The reason it's good is because it protects a scene from being trite [see fig. 17]. Because it is exposition. It's like dressing up a scene a little bit with counterpoint. There were times that I didn't write it that way, or I wrote it straight, and then the counterpoint developed in the staging. My most fun was putting the stuff on its feet. Writing it is wonderful, and you're the only one that has the absolute image in your brain of what you've written. No matter how may times a stranger reads it, they haven't the faintest idea where it's going to go. They think what's written is what they're going to see. Which is the case in most movies: you read a scene, go to the movie, it's *exact!* Uh-uh. I think I had maybe three or four exacts in my life that I directed. Only in that I've always written knowing the writer is going to be taken in the hands of the director and he's going to rise above that material. I always knew that. And even with that—I wish you could see a couple of my scripts, shooting scripts, and see the material as written versus what you remember on the screen. You will see the connection. It's not so that when you see it you won't recognize it; you'll know it immediately. But you will see where I take it. If I couldn't take that, I wouldn't use it. It's that simple. If I couldn't enhance it, I wouldn't use it.

CF: Would you say that you deliberately wrote a little loose, to give yourself that room?

Figure 17. Counterpoint: Kathleen Freeman and Jerry Lewis in *The Ladies Man.*

JL: Exactly. Exactly. That's a perfect word. By not snugging it up, and it became vital to read it that way. I couldn't work that way anyhow. And every director I ever worked with, including Scorsese, said, "Please open it up." You know, any good director wants you the actor to rise above the written word. And to give an actor that freedom, he'll go on his ass many times, and a good actor very often doesn't want that. "Hey, I learned it this way. Don't you want what I've learned?" "Yep, if that's what you want to do, perfect. No problem." A director knows immediately, let's get what I got on the page. When an actor says, "I'm so thrilled that it's loose," you got paydirt. At least the actor will take it to a couple of places that might be viable, and if he takes it into the toilet, he's courageous enough to go there again. You do that, it's wonderful. You're not going to die. No one's going to kill your children. When you see a film being made with a director that's so stoic, so tight, and so committed to the granite written material, that's not fun. You'll get great actors to do that for you, but then you'll have that very stoic, tight film.

William Wyler had that wonderful ability to take static pages and bring them to life. He did it with staging. Wyler was a master at staging a scene. If you look at *The Best Years of Our Lives,* God almighty, what a beautifully directed movie. You know why I knew how good it was? I was jealous. I always know when something's superior. That's the wonderful part of our business, Chris: those of us who are presumed to be excellent in their work are the last ones to know how good they are. You know, I hate to make that admission, because it feels like a sign of weakness, but that's what we are. Imagine this. I'm sitting with a man like Elie Wiesel, who, I mean, you sit with him, you're like sitting with God, he's so wonderful. I said to Elie one day, "I'm not ashamed to tell you that I need to get before an audience. And that I'm envious of you that do not. Because I'm not as happy in my life." This was before Sam [SanDee, Lewis's second wife, whom he married in 1983] and my daughter, of course. But I was telling him, years ago, "I'm not happy in my life unless I'm in front of an audience." He said, "Do you know the why of that?" I said, "Yes, I do know the why of that. I am love-hungry, and I have eight hundred mommies and daddies going [claps hands] 'Good Jerry.'" That's what actors are doing. They need to show off. They need to take what they believe is a viable or interesting part of their chemistry, their talent, they need to go and present it. And then after it's presented, they need the adulation.

CF: It was important to you to show this in your films, to deal with this dynamic and need directly.

JL: And a lot of times I didn't know I did it. It's people like you that fuck up my life who tell me you saw that, you know. But it's wonderful because, imagine this. I did a lot of this work forty to fifty years ago. And I'm sitting today in the year 2003 with a young man, young enough to be my son, who knows my work as well as I do, and yet he's going to bring a spirit to me by his recollections that I never dreamed would be possible. But you have no idea what that means to someone who yearns to know that what he did was good. It's marvelous. You're not going to get this admission from a lot of people, because a lot of people won't dig down and go there. I don't have a problem with it. I don't believe you're going to think of me as a man that's demeaned by it, and I don't believe you're going to think I'm weak by it. But it's true. And because it's true, and you understand that dynamic, then everything else you're talking about you'll understand even that much better. . . .

I know Jerry, I sleep with him, remember? I know him, I know that son-of-a-bitch in and out. I know his needs, I know that without him I wouldn't have food on the table. He works for me and very well. When I talk about him in the third person, people look at you askance. Are you fuckin' schizophrenic? Yes, in the creative, yes. I can talk to you much better about Jerry, being the creator of him, and I'm going to be seventy-eight years old—we're talking about the nine-year-old. The nine-year-old within me. I have no compunction about telling everything I know about him. I don't have a problem about that. I'm not going to sit down with you and say, "Good morning, would you like a drink, and oh, by the way, the depth of my soul. . . ." That's not how it works. You wait to hear what the man wants. And if it's interesting, and if he clicks in, one with his personality, two with his concern, and three his care, I go through the fucking wall. I do.

CF: In *The Patsy*, Hedda Hopper says: "You've come across somebody who hasn't yet learned to be phony. He felt something, and he said it, which was real and honest. And now if you apply that to his performance, you've got a great success."

JL: I believe it. I've gotten further with truth than a thousand people hedging, fudging. When you learn, and I have, truth is immediate. Now. Faster than now. A lie takes a week, and then you've got to remember the son of a bitch. Most of the characters that I played had truth as a foundation. Rarely would you see one of them deceptive for deceptive's sake. Cagey, maybe; cunning, maybe. Never deceptive. His truth was part of his innocence. And certainly part of his naivety.

CF: Is that still true in *Three on a Couch*, where he plays the three roles?

JL: In that deception, it was survival. That deception had to prevail for the movie to work. You know, I wrote that with Sam Taylor. It was kind of a stretch because I couldn't get Jerry out there. He wouldn't come. I hoped he would, but he wouldn't come. Not in that frame.

CF: You're not credited as a writer on that.

JL: No.

CF: But you did work extensively on the script?

JL: With the condition that there be no credit. And I was fine with that. Sam Taylor was a very established writer. He never had worked with anyone, and didn't mind, because he knew I was creative. And he didn't know a hell of a lot about Jerry and his ability. So we worked together very well.

CF: To get back to your point about truth. How does that apply to the story of *The Nutty Professor,* where you have a man who becomes somebody else? What is the truth that comes out of that?

JL: That there is good and bad in everyone. And since I was a kid, I was never frightened at Jekyll and Hyde. I saw Fredric March, I think, was he the first? I was a kid.

CF: 1932.

JL: So I'm five, six years old. But my recollection is when I'm older. My recollection is around nine, and it's a good recollection. I'm sitting there, and it was a rerun, it was called Popular Demand Rerun at the local theater near where I lived, and on Wednesday nights they had Popular Demand Reruns, which is the theater's way of saving on rentals, you know. Only one night. Three shows. Six, eight, ten, something like that. I watched them all. I watched the three performances. And I'm telling you, I giggled throughout. Because I put myself in my clown mask and watched it as a comic. I wanted to see if . . . my belief at that time, and being so young, though I had already learned through my dad's work and my wonderful discussions with him, was that comedy laughter and painful hate are really two factions that rub against one another. That laughter is the reverse side of despair. But when you have one man with two sides, one is good and one is bad, it's the same premise, in a sense. I watched the transformation and what he did, and for me it was funny when he was chased down the street by the police jumping over a fence. That classy gentleman, who was gonna marry this lovely lady, doesn't jump over a fuckin' fence, which you know is done by the stunt man, 'cause the son-of-a-bitch was seven feet tall. Seven foot tall, and he jumped it. Well, I got hysterical. And that giggle took me through his panic of, "Oh, God, I gotta drink the potion."

I'm now talking about from the age, let's say I was ten, for round numbers, okay, because I guess at about ten I had the mentality to examine, why do I like it that way instead of that way? I didn't think that of *[I Am a] Fugitive from a Chain Gang,* I didn't think that in *Public Enemy Number One*, I didn't think about it in *Little Caesar,* I didn't think that in *Wuthering Heights,* you know. Why that? So I started to find out as much as I could twenty years later, at the age of around thirty. Dean and I had just split up. I was just thirty in '56. And my mind started going about that project. I researched Robert Louis Stevenson as far as I could go. [Robert] Benayoun helped me with that research. He was supposed to have had a wonderful sense of humor. But whether he did or he didn't, it was very apparent to me this was very serious writing about a very, very serious notion that affected every man in the world. If he took it to be identifiable to him, he would understand it, I think. Though there would be the man who says, "I'm one person. I'm a nice man, and that's all I am." It stuck with me. For the next four years, I really started to write. I wrote nine screenplays and shot the first. I kept polishing a turd. I once said to a musician, "You can't polish a turd." He said, "You can if you freeze it." That's what I was doing. When I got ready to make it, I went forward with the first writing. 'Cause I thought it was perfect. But I wish you could see scripts two, three, four, down to nine. I mean, they just got progressively worse. No rhythm, no continuity, exposition was missing. I mean, I was looking to do things, and . . . that wasn't me. I don't write and edit. I write in original moments. Now, if I try to edit it, I screw it up. If I repair grammar, that's no problem, my girls do that.

CF: Was it because you were intimidated by the size of the theme that you went through all these redundant drafts?

JL: Very possible. Because I knew I was taking on a heavy-duty classic, and will I be accused of ridiculing it. . . . When it came time to do it, you've seen the board for shooting, haven't you? Day, add a day, add a day? I took everything of Buddy Love and put it here. So that I had twenty-five days of the professor. After the twenty-fifth shooting day, I meet Buddy Love now. I procrastinated up to the very day that I had to get him dressed. I hated it. There's scenes I can show you where you see it. I hated playing him. What'd I tell you about a writer: he tips his mitt when he writes something, doesn't he? I was really concerned that I knew the depth of that ill-mannered son of a bitch. How do I know that? Am I like that to know that? My sons would say to me, "You're not like that to know that. You're a very intelligent man, you've got an IQ of 179, for Christ's sakes, you know about people." They're trying to convince me that I'm not really getting into this terrible rut of, "How did I know that?" You know, Stephen King writes something that's vicious; doesn't mean he does that, but how does he know about it? I always ask that question. I didn't play Buddy until the twenty-eighth shooting day, and then I had to do it.

You know the thing that really distressed the shit out of me, the people that said, "Was that your, ah, your shot at your ex-partner?" I said, "What the fuck are you talking about? I loved my partner. He's not ex, he's my partner. I loved him as much as I do my daughter. What's the matter with you?" "Well, we thought you were just gettin' even." I said, "Well, you have to think what you think. But if you want to know, I'll tell you what I wrote. I wrote about the man that takes a potion that turns him into Monster. But a monster that's among us, not a monster in the jungle. And the monster among us is coarse, crass, ill-mannered, ill-tempered, intolerant, pushy, crass, abrasive, loud, caustic. That's the guy I want to write. That's what the beautiful little chemist becomes. That was the whole notion. My partner would never look or act anything like that." But anyhow when I explained it, everyone seemed to go, [dryly] "Oh, I see. Okay, thank you." I'm going to go to everyone's home that saw the movie and explain this, right? But that was exactly my explanation, because that's exactly what I was doing. If I had a mean streak in me and I wanted to attack my partner, I could do it much better than that.

I didn't have to disguise it, you know. I was offended that people would think I would do that, but they don't know me, so they're going to think anything. But anyhow, I loved what I was able to see in the end result. I made the movie I wanted to make. No regrets. If I shot it tomorrow, I don't know that I would do it a hell of a lot differently. I might refine some moves, I might tighten some things, I might delete a couple of things, maybe add a couple of things. But on the whole, if they said, "Will you let this be the way it is for perpetuity?" I'd say, yeah, I'm very happy with it. I am.

CF: It's certainly a great film. What strikes me about Buddy Love is that he's not all bad, and the audience is on his side a lot.

JL: You'd be amazed at the mail he got. From women. Handsome, debonair, so charming. I'm thinking, What fucking movie did they see? Charming? Uh, sexy, great command, great presence? I'm trying to write a moron, you know.

CF: But the character is sympathetic at certain moments.

JL: Like where?

CF: The second time he comes into the Purple Pit, he's already drunk, which is not attractive, but you start to look at the character a little differently, you say, this guy has a real problem. He's not just somebody who from a position from complete superiority and egomania pushes everybody else around. He's a guy who's troubled and has a drinking problem because of it. And then you see him play the piano, alone with Stella, and you say, "Well, he's pretty sensitive, that he can play it that way."

JL: Well, part of that was the Professor within him. I always had to keep the core within the Professor. Though we didn't see that come out in Buddy Love. Because we couldn't; it would be totally confusing. But we did know that he had sensitivity enough in both characters, to feel for both characters. He had to know what Buddy did the night before, though he didn't consciously know what he did. That gave me a couple of pretty good pauses, how to deal with that. I remember one day I screamed out loud—my son Ron was on the boat—I said, "Help me, God help me, I'm so mixed up. Read this." So I let him read a couple of pages. He said, "It's pretty clear to me, Dad." I said, "It is?" I read it again, I said, "Yeah, I guess so." You see, when his voice cracked, on the cliff in the love scene, he had to know as the Professor that he was getting into trouble. Or, as Buddy he had to know he was getting in trouble. So, I tried to keep them so distant they knew nothing of one another, except when they were confronted, like the next morning, he remembered by what she said, not by what he recalled. So it became . . . picture that kind of a tennis match. Well, he knew that. No, he didn't know. Oh, okay, but he understood. No. She said it. He accepted it. He had to. He didn't have an argument for her. "Oh, what happened with you last night, professor?" Oh, w . . . [gibbering] Huh?

CF: Buddy Love is also sympathetic because the audience loves him.

JL: Yes, which I didn't believe would happen.

CF: But also the onscreen audience. He's an immediate sensation at the Purple Pit [see fig. 18]. And you've got that closeup of Stella Stevens, so gorgeously lit . . .

JL: She was gorgeous.

CF: And she looks at him with something like love, at that moment.

JL: Yeah.

CF: So it's hard not to positively toward the character, no matter how many negative traits he has, when you see he generates such love.

JL: The character had the ability to have you forget the ugliness when he was in the present form of pleasantness. I can't take credit for that, but that's what the audience did. They left the Polar-Bear Heater

Figure 18. *The Nutty Professor:* Buddy Love
(Jerry Lewis) at the Purple Pit

at the bar when he was talking with some degree of reality for a moment or two. I think he said to a waitress, "Get me the drink, move it," but then he softened. I think that people understood the peaks and valleys of the character. I wish I could tell you I built him on peaks and valleys. I didn't. I built him strictly with one point of view. All of those things he is, I gotta have that.

CF: He also says something that's very true in the scene on the cliff with Stella Stevens. First he's, "Wipe off the lipstick, let's get started."

JL: Right. That's my favorite Buddy Love scene.

CF: But then he tries a different approach, and he says, "You know darn well that everyone likes to be loved, admired." And that's perfectly true, and that's said in different ways in your other films, and which you must believe.

JL: Yes, oh, I do, of course. You saw evidence of that from me as the man, in this set of circumstances.

Note

1. Lewis is describing something he also put in a film: in the airplane scene in *Cracking Up,* the flight attendant offers Warren (Lewis) a pornographic flip book in lieu of an inflight movie.

Films and Television Programs Directed by Jerry Lewis

The Bellboy (1960)
Producer: Jerry Lewis (Jerry Lewis Pictures)
Distributor: Paramount
Director: Jerry Lewis
Screenplay: Jerry Lewis
Photography: Haskell Boggs
Art Directors: Hal Pereira, Henry Bumstead
Editor: Stanley Johnson
Music: Walter Scharf
Cast: Jerry Lewis (Stanley/Jerry Lewis), Alex Gerry (Mr. Novak), Bob Clayton (Bob), Bill Richmond ("Stan Laurel"), Milton Berle (Himself/Bellboy), Cary Middlecoff (Himself), Herkie Styles, Sonny Sands, Eddie Shaeffer, David Landfield (Bellboys), Jimmy Gerard, Matilda Gerard (Fighting couple), Jack Kruschen (Jack Emulsion), Walter Winchell (Voiceover narrator), The Novelites (Themselves), B. S. Pully, Maxie Rosenbloom, Joe E. Ross (Gangsters), Larry Best (Apple man), Roy Sedley (Man at pool), Jack Durant (Mr. Manville), Guy Rennie (Mr. Carter)
Black and white
72 min.

The Ladies Man (1961)
Producer: Jerry Lewis (York Pictures)
Distributor: Paramount
Director: Jerry Lewis
Screenplay: Jerry Lewis, Bill Richmond
Photography: W. Wallace Kelley
Art Directors: Hal Pereira, Ross Bellah
Editor: Stanley Johnson
Music: Walter Scharf

Cast: Jerry Lewis (Herbert H. Heebert/Herbert's mother), Helen Traubel (Helen Wellenmelon), Kathleen Freeman (Katie), Pat Stanley (Fay), Buddy Lester (Willard C. Gainsborough), George Raft (Himself), Hope Holiday (Miss Anxious), Lynn Ross (Miss Vitality), Sylvia Lewis (Miss Cartilage), Madlyn Rhue (Miss Intellect), Harry James and His Orchestra (Themselves), Westbrook Van Voorhis (Himself), Alex Gerry (TV producer), Doodles Weaver (Sound man), Jack Kruschen (Graduation emcee), Kenneth MacDonald (Herbert's father), Beverly Wills (Miss Hypochondriac), Ann McCrea (Miss Sexy Pot), Caroline Richter (Miss Southern Accent), Mary La Roche, Daria Massey, Lillian Briggs, Patricia Blair, Francesca Bellini (Boarders), Vicki Benet (French singer), Del Moore (Announcer), Mary LeBow (French maid)
Technicolor
106 min.

Permanent Waves (1962?)
Unsold TV pilot.
Director: Jerry Lewis
Cast: Hope Holiday, Kathleen Freeman
25 min. (approx.)

The Errand Boy (1962)
Producer: Ernest D. Glucksman (Jerry Lewis Productions)
Distributor: Paramount
Director: Jerry Lewis
Screenplay: Jerry Lewis, Bill Richmond
Photography: W. Wallace Kelley
Art Director: Hal Pereira, Arthur Lonergan
Editor: Stanley E. Johnson
Music: Walter Scharf
Cast: Jerry Lewis (Morty S. Tashman/Second poster hanger), Brian Donlevy (Tom Paramutual), Howard McNear (Mr. Sneak), Stanley Adams (Mailroom manager), Dick Wesson (Assistant director), Robert Ivers (New York director), Pat Dahl (Miss Carson), Renée Taylor (Miss Giles), Rita Hayes (Singer), Isobel Elsom (Irma Paramutual), Sig Ruman (Baron), Kathleen Freeman (Helen Paramutual), Iris Adrian (Anastasia), Fritz Feld (Buzzbie), Felicia Atkins (Serina), Doodles Weaver (Weaver), Kenneth MacDonald (Fumble), Joey Forman (Jedson), Paul and Mary Ritts (Magnolia marionettists), Milton Frome (Mr. Greenback), Dave Landfield (Lance), Del Moore (Himself), Benny Rubin (Mr. Wabenlottnee), Regis Toomey (Man in projection room), Richard Bakalyan (Director), William Wellman Jr. (Star in love scene), Dan Blocker, Lorne Greene, Michael Landon, Pernell Roberts (Themselves), the Dover Basketeers (Basketball

players), Joe Besser (Man in projection room), Mike Mazurki (Stunt man in blond wig), Bill Richmond (Monocled man in elevator), Mike Ross (Man in elevator), Mary Treen (Commissary cashier), Herbert Vigran (Cigar smoker in elevator)
Black and white
92 min.

The Nutty Professor (1963)
Producer: Ernest D. Glucksman (Jerry Lewis Productions)
Distributor: Paramount
Director: Jerry Lewis
Screenplay: Jerry Lewis, Bill Richmond
Photography: W. Wallace Kelley
Art Directors: Hal Pereira, Walter Tyler
Editor: John Woodcock
Music: Walter Scharf
Cast: Jerry Lewis (Professor Julius Kelp/Buddy Love/Kelp as baby), Stella Stevens (Stella), Del Moore (Dr. Warfield), Kathleen Freeman (Miss Lemon), Howard Morris (Elmer Kelp), Elvia Allman (Edwina Kelp), Henry Gibson (Gibson), Med Flory (Worshefski), Norman Alden, Julie Parrish, Skip Ward, David Landfield, Francine York, Celeste Yarnall (Students), Milton Frome (Dr. M. Sheppard Leevee), Buddy Lester (Bartender), Les Brown and His Band of Renown (Themselves), Murray Alper (Gym attendant), Michael Ross (Weightlifter), Richard Kiel, Hugh Cannon (Tall men in gym), Gavin Gordon (Clothes salesman)
Technicolor
107 min.

The Patsy (1964)
Producer: Ernest D. Glucksman (Jerry Lewis Productions/Patti Enterprises)
Distributor: Paramount
Director: Jerry Lewis
Screenplay: Jerry Lewis, Bill Richmond
Photography: W. Wallace Kelley
Art Directors: Hal Pereira, Carey O'Dell
Editors: John Woodcock, Arthur P. Schmidt
Music: David Raksin
Cast: Jerry Lewis (Stanley Belt), Ina Balin (Ellen Betz), Everett Sloane (Caryl Ferguson), Phil Harris (Chic Wymore), Keenan Wynn (Harry Silver), John Carradine (Bruce Arden), Peter Lorre (Morgan Heywood), Hans Conreid (Professor Mueller), Richard Deacon (Sy Devore), Phil Foster (Mayo Sloan), Del Moore (Policeman), Nancy Kulp (Helen), Hedda Hopper, Ed Sullivan, Ed Wynn, Mel Torme, Rhonda Fleming, Lloyd Thaxton,

George Raft, the Step Brothers (Themselves), Benny Rubin (Waiter), Fritz Feld (Maître d'), Dick Bakalyan, Norman Alden, Robert Ivers (Men at dance), Scatman Crothers (Shoeshine), Neil Hamilton (Barber), Lorraine Crawford (Manicurist), Bill Richmond (Pianist), Mantan Moreland (Barbershop porter), Quinn O'Hara (Cigarette girl), Richard Gehman, Vernon Scott (Themselves)
Technicolor
101 min.

"A Little Fun to Match the Sorrow" (1965)
Episode of the TV series *Ben Casey*
Producer: Wilton Schiller (Bing Crosby Productions)
Broadcasting network: ABC-TV
Director: Jerry Lewis
Teleplay: Chester Krumholz
Photography: Ted Voigtlander
Art Director: Rolland M. Brooks
Editor: Mike Pozen
Music: Johnny Williams
Cast: Vincent Edwards (Dr. Ben Casey), Jerry Lewis (Dr. Dennis Green), Dianne Foster (Karen Fischer), Sam Jaffe (Dr. Zorba), Harry Landers (Dr. Ted Hoffman), Bettye Ackerman (Dr. Maggie Graham), Jeanne Bates (Miss Wills), James Best (Dr. Joe Sullivan), Tige Andrews (Dave McClusky), Robert H. Harris (Mr. Burns), Svea Grunfeld (Helen Fenton), Todd Garretson (Larry)
Black and white
52 min.

The Family Jewels (1965)
Producer: Jerry Lewis (Jerry Lewis Enterprises)
Distributor: Paramount
Director: Jerry Lewis
Screenplay: Jerry Lewis, Bill Richmond
Photography: W. Wallace Kelley
Art Directors: Hal Pereira, Jack Poplin
Editor: John Woodcock
Music: Pete King
Cast: Jerry Lewis (Willard Woodward/Bugsy Peyton/James Peyton/Everett Peyton/Julius Peyton/Captain Eddie Peyton/Skylock Peyton), Donna Butterworth (Donna Peyton), Sebastian Cabot (Dr. Matson), Neil Hamilton, Jay Adler (Attorneys), Robert Strauss (Pool hustler), Gene Baylos (Circus clown), Marjorie Bennett, Ellen Corby, Renie Riano, Jesslyn Fax, Frances Lax (Airplane passengers), Anne Baxter (Hostess),

Del Moore (Butler), Gerald Mohr, William Wellman Jr. (Dinner guests), Bill Richmond (Cab driver), Vince Barnett (Man with antique car), Gary Lewis and the Playboys (Themselves), Milton Frome (Pilot), Benny Rubin (Sign painter), Herbie Faye (Joe), John Lawrence (Chief petty officer), Francine York (Airline hostess), John Hubbard (Pilot), Michael Ross (Guard), Douglas Deane (Model)
Technicolor
100 min.

Three on a Couch (1966)
Producer: Jerry Lewis (Jerry Lewis Productions)
Distributor: Columbia
Director: Jerry Lewis
Screenplay: Bob Ross, Samuel A. Taylor, based on a story by Arne Sultan and Marvin Worth
Photography: W. Wallace Kelley, Robert Bronner
Art Director: Leo K. Kuter
Editor: Russel Wiles
Music: Louis Brown
Cast: Jerry Lewis (Christopher Pride/Warren/Ringo Raintree/Rutherford/ Heather), Janet Leigh (Dr. Elizabeth Acord), James Best (Dr. Ben Mizer), Mary Ann Mobley (Susan Manning), Gila Golan (Anna Jacque), Leslie Parrish (Mary Lou Mauve), Kathleen Freeman (Murphy), Buddy Lester (Drunk), Renzo Cesana (Ambassador), Fritz Feld (Attaché), Danny Costello (Singer), Renie Riano (Green Stamps)
Pathecolor
109 min.

The Big Mouth (1967)
Producer: Jerry Lewis (Jerry Lewis Productions)
Distributor: Columbia
Director: Jerry Lewis
Screenplay: Jerry Lewis, Bill Richmond, based on a story by Bill Richmond
Photography: W. Wallace Kelley
Art Director: Lyle Wheeler
Editor: Russel Wiles
Music: Harry Betts
Cast: Jerry Lewis (Gerald Clamson/Sid Valentine), Susan Bay (Suzie Cartwright), Harold J. Stone (Thor), Charlie Callas (Rex), Buddy Lester (Studs), Del Moore (Mr. Hodges), Jeannine Riley (Bambi Berman), Leonard Stone (Fong), John Nolan (Webster), Paul Lambert (Moxie), Frank De Vol (Narrator), Vern Rowe (Gunner), Dave Lipp (Lizard), Vincent Van Lynn (Fancher), Mike Mahoney, Walter Kray (Detectives),

Eddie Ryder (Specs), Colonel Harland Sanders (Himself), William
Wellman Jr. (Harold), George Takei (Worker in Fong's lab), Florence Lake
(Little old lady), Vince Barnett (Man at phone booth)
Pathecolor
107 min.

One More Time (1970)
Producer: Milton Ebbins (ChrisLaw-Trace-Mark)
Distributor: United Artists
Director: Jerry Lewis
Screenplay: Michael Pertwee
Photography: Ernest W. Steward
Production Designer: Jack Stevens
Editor: Bill Butler
Music: Les Reed
Cast: Sammy Davis Jr. (Charlie Salt), Peter Lawford (Chris Pepper/Lord
Sydney Pepper), Maggie Wright (Miss Tomkins), Leslie Sands (Inspector
Crock), John Wood (Figg), Sydney Arnold (Tombs), Edward Evans
(Gordon), Percy Herbert (Mander), Dudley Sutton (Wilson), Esther
Anderson (Billie), Anthony Nicholls (Candler), Allan Cuthbertson
(Belton), Moultrie Kelsall (Minister), Glyn Owen (Dennis), Lucille Soong
(Kim Lee), Cyril Luckham (Magistrate), Bill Maynard (Jenson), David
Trevena (Gene Abernathy), Norman Mitchell (Sergeant Smith), Richard
Goolden (Ninth local), Joanna Wake (Claire Turpington-Mellish), Julian
D'Albie (Lord Turpington-Mellish), Gladys Spencer (Lady Turpington-
Mellish), Geoffrey Morris (Police doctor), Norman Pitt, George McGrath
(Country gentlemen), Mischa De La Motte (Maître d'), Walter Horsbrugh
(Clerk of the court), John Nettles (Dixon), Peter Reeves (Policeman),
Juliette Bora, Florence George, Lorraine Hall, Thelma Neal, Amber
Dean Smith, Carmel Stratton (Salt and Pepper Girls), Peter Cushing (Dr.
Frankenstein), Christopher Lee (Dracula)
DeLuxe Color
93 min.

Which Way to the Front? (1970)
Producer: Jerry Lewis (Jerry Lewis Productions)
Distributor: Warner Bros.
Director: Jerry Lewis
Screenplay: Gerald Gardner, Dee Caruso, from a story by Gerald Gardner
Photography: W. Wallace Kelley
Art Director: John Beckman
Editor: Russel Wiles
Music: Louis Y. Brown

Cast: Jerry Lewis (Brendan Byers III/Field Marshal Eric Kesselring), Jan
Murray (Sid Hackle), John Wood (Finkel), Steve Franken (Peter Bland),
Dack Rambo (Terry Love), Sidney Miller (Adolf Hitler), Robert Middleton
(Colonico), Willie Davis (Lincoln), Kaye Ballard (Mayor's wife), Harold J.
Stone (General Buck), Paul Winchell (Schroeder), Myron Healey (Major),
Fritz Feld (Von Runstadt), Joe Besser (Dock Master), Danny Dayton
(Man in car), Bobo Lewis (Bland's wife), Kathleen Freeman (Bland's
mother), George Takei (Yamashita), Martin Kosleck (German submarine
commander), Benny Rubin (Field marshal in conspiracy), Mike Mazurki
(Rocky), William Wellman Jr. (Mosgrove), Ronald Lewis (Lieutenant
Levitch), Neil Hamilton (Chief of staff), Bob Lauher (Sergeant), Milton
Frome (Executive), Gary Crosby, Artie Lewis, Mickey Manners (SS
guards), Kenneth MacDonald (Admiral), Herbert Vigran (Officer), Henry
Corden (Thug), Richard Loo, Teru Shimada (Japanese naval officers)
Technicolor
96 min.

"In Dreams They Run" (1970)
Episode of the TV series *The Bold Ones (The New Doctors)*
Producer: Joel Rogosin (Harbour Productions Unlimited/UTV)
Broadcasting network: NBC-TV
Director: Jerry Lewis
Teleplay: Don Tait, Sandy Stern, from a story by Don Tait
Photography: Gerald Perry Finnerman
Art Director: John E. Chilberg, II
Editor: Budd Small
Music: Dave Grusin
Cast: John Saxon (Dr. Theodore Stuart), E. G. Marshall (Dr. David Craig),
David Hartman (Dr. Paul Hunter), Joanne Linville (Anne Sorenson),
Arch Johnson (Frank Sorenson), Lincoln Kilpatrick (Gil Dodds), Ella
Edwards (Babe Dodds), Jason Karpf (Davey Sorenson), Del Moore
(Announcer), Robbie MacDonald (Warren McRae), Anne Whitfield
(Milly), Kathleen Freeman, Eve Brent, Cecile Ozorio, Alyscia Maxwell,
Christine Nelson (Nurses)
Color
55 min.

Hardly Working (1980)
Producers: James J. McNamara, Igo Kantor
Distributor: Twentieth Century–Fox
Director: Jerry Lewis
Screenplay: Michael Janover, Jerry Lewis, from an original story by Michael
Janover

Photography: James Pergola
Art Director: Don Ivey
Editor: Michael Luciano
Music: Morton Stevens
Cast: Jerry Lewis (Bo Hooper/Woman outside hotel), Susan Oliver (Claire Trent), Roger C. Carmel (Robert Trent), Deanna Lund (Millie), Harold J. Stone (Frank Loucazi), Steve Franken (Steve Torres), Buddy Lester (Claude Reed), Leonard Stone (Ted Mitchell), Jerry Lester (Slats), Billy Barty (Sammy), Alex Hentelhoff (J. Balling), Britt Leach (Gas station manager), Peggy Mondo (Woman in restaurant), Amy Krug (Michele Trent), Steven Baccus (Peter), Tommy Zibelli II (Bobby Trent), Buffy Dee (C.B.), Lou Marsh (Tony the clown), Tony Adams (Eddie the clown), Bob May (Clown), Angela Bomford (Curio lady), Jack McDermott (Banker), Cary Hoffman (Waiter), Jack Wakefield (Disco manager), Jordana Wester (Lady in house), John Rice, Greg Rice (Midget clowns), SanDee Pitnick (Disco dancer)
Color
91 min.

Cracking Up (Smorgasbord; 1983)
Producers: Peter Nelson, Arnold Orgolini (Orgolini-Nelson Productions)
Distributor: Warner Bros.
Director: Jerry Lewis
Screenplay: Jerry Lewis, Bill Richmond
Photography: Gerald Perry Finnerman
Production Designer: Tracy Bousman
Set Designers: Elizabeth Bousman, Richard McKenzie, Robert Bacon
Editor: Gene Fowler Jr.
Music: Morton Stevens
Cast: Jerry Lewis (Warren Nefron/Jacques Nefron/Warren's father/Bank robber/Dr. Peck), Herb Edelman (Dr. Jonas Pletchick), Foster Brooks (Pilot), Zane Buzby (Waitress/Valet), Dick Butkus (Antismoking therapist), Francine York (Marie Du Bois), John Abbott (Surgeon), Bill Richmond (Schoolmate/Driver), Buddy Lester (Passenger), Milton Berle (Woman patient), Sammy Davis Jr. (Himself), Michael Ross (Prison guard)
Color
89 min.

"Boy" (1990)
Episode in *How Are the Kids? / Comment vont les enfants?*
Producer: C91 Communications
Director: Jerry Lewis
Screenplay: Jerry Lewis

Photography: Mike McGowan, John Winner
Editors: Roy Benson, Larry Moten
Music: George Delerue
Cast: Isaac Lidsky, Ivory Sommers, Bob Thompson, Virginia Thompson
Color
8 min.

Other Films Starring Jerry Lewis

This list contains only the theatrical feature films in which Jerry Lewis appears in a principal role. Cameo appearances and TV appearances are not represented. Films produced by Lewis's production companies are marked by an asterisk (*).

My Friend Irma (1949)
Director: George Marshall
Producer: Hal B. Wallis (Paramount)

My Friend Irma Goes West (1950)
Director: Hal Walker
Producer: Hal B. Wallis (Paramount)

At War with the Army (1950)*
Director: Hal Walker
Producers: Fred F. Finklehoffe, Abner J. Greshler (York Pictures)

That's My Boy (1951)
Director: Hal Walker
Producer: Hal B. Wallis (Paramount)

Sailor Beware (1951)
Director: Hal Walker
Producer: Hal B. Wallis (Paramount)

Jumping Jacks (1952)
Director: Norman Taurog
Producer: Hal B. Wallis (Paramount)

The Stooge (1953)
Director: Norman Taurog
Producer: Hal B. Wallis (Paramount)

Scared Stiff (1953)
Director: George Marshall
Producer: Hal B. Wallis (Paramount)

The Caddy (1953)°
Director: Norman Taurog
Producer: Paul Jones (York Pictures)

Money from Home (1954)
Director: George Marshall
Producer: Hal B. Wallis (Paramount)
Special material in song numbers staged by Jerry Lewis

Living It Up (1954)°
Director: Norman Taurog
Producer: Paul Jones (York Pictures)

Three-Ring Circus (1954)
Director: Joseph Pevney
Producer: Hal B. Wallis (Paramount)

You're Never Too Young (1955)°
Director: Norman Taurog
Producer: Paul Jones (York Pictures)

Artists and Models (1955)
Director: Frank Tashlin
Producer: Hal B. Wallis (Paramount)

Pardners (1956)°
Director: Norman Taurog
Producer: Paul Jones (York Pictures)

Hollywood or Bust (1956)
Director: Frank Tashlin
Producer: Hal B. Wallis (Paramount)

The Delicate Delinquent (1957)°
Director: Don McGuire
Producer: Jerry Lewis (York Pictures)

The Sad Sack (1957)
Director: George Marshall
Producer: Hal B. Wallis (Paramount)

Rock-a-Bye Baby (1958)°
Director: Frank Tashlin
Producer: Jerry Lewis (York Pictures)

The Geisha Boy (1958)°
Director: Frank Tashlin
Producer: Jerry Lewis (York Pictures)

Don't Give Up the Ship (1959)
Director: Norman Taurog
Producer: Hal B. Wallis (Paramount)

Visit to a Small Planet (1960)
Director: Norman Taurog
Producer: Hal B. Wallis (Paramount)

Cinderfella (1960)°
Director: Frank Tashlin
Producer: Jerry Lewis (Jerry Lewis Pictures)

It's Only Money (1962)°
Director: Frank Tashlin
Producer: Jerry Lewis (York Pictures/Jerry Lewis Productions)

Who's Minding the Store? (1963)°
Director: Frank Tashlin
Producer: Jerry Lewis (York Pictures/Jerry Lewis Productions)

The Disorderly Orderly (1964)°
Director: Frank Tashlin
Producer: Paul Jones (York Pictures/Jerry Lewis Productions)

Boeing Boeing (1965)
Director: John Rich
Producer: Hal B. Wallis (Paramount)

Way . . . Way Out (1966)°
Director: Gordon Douglas
Producer: Malcolm Stuart (Jerry Lewis Productions/Coldwater Productions/
    Way Out Co.)

Don't Raise the Bridge, Lower the River (1968)
Director: Jerry Paris
Producer: Walter Shenson (Walter Shenson Productions)

Hook, Line, and Sinker (1969)°
Director: George Marshall
Producer: Jerry Lewis (Jerry Lewis Productions)

The King of Comedy (1983)
Director: Martin Scorsese
Producer: Arnon Milchan (Embassy International Pictures)

Slapstick (of Another Kind) (1984)
Director: Steven Paul
Producer: Steven Paul (International Film Marketing)

Retenez moi . . . ou je fais un malheur (Hold me back or I'll have an accident;
    1984)
Director: Michel Gérard
Producers: Pierre Kalfon, Michel Gérard (Imacité/Coline)

Par où t'es rentré? On t'as pas vu sortir (How did you get in? We didn't see
    you leave; 1984)
Director: Philippe Clair
Producer: Tarak Ben Ammar (Carthago)

Arizona Dream (1993)
Director: Emir Kusturica
Producers: Yves Marmion, Claudie Ossard (Canal+/Constellation/Hachette
    Première/UGC)

Funny Bones (1995)
Director: Peter Chelsom
Producers: Peter Chelsom, Simon Fields (Hollywood Pictures)

The following represents a small selection from the vast literature on Lewis. Extensive bibliographies can be found in the books by Benayoun, Krutnik, and Levy.

Aumont, Jacques, Jean-Louis Comolli, André S. Labarthe, Jean Narboni, and Sylvie Pierre. "Petit lexique des termes lewisiens." *Cahiers du cinéma* 197 (December 1967/January 1968): 58–63.

Benayoun, Robert. *Bonjour Monsieur Lewis.* Paris: Eric Losfeld, 1972.

Blanchot, Maurice. *The Infinite Conversation.* Trans. Susan Hanson. Minneapolis: University of Minnesota Press, 1993.

———. "Literature and the Right to Death." In *The Station Hill Blanchot Reader: Fiction and Literary Essays.* Ed. George Quasha. Trans. Lydia Davis. Barrytown, N.Y.: Station Hill Press, 1999. 359–99.

Bogdanovich, Peter. *Pieces of Time: Peter Bogdanovich on the Movies.* New York: Arbor House, 1973.

———. *Who the Hell's in It: Portraits and Conversations.* New York: Alfred A. Knopf, 2004.

Bukatman, Scott. "Paralysis in Motion: Jerry Lewis's Life as a Man." In *Comedy/Cinema/Theory.* Ed. Andrew S. Horton. Berkeley: University of California Press, 1991. 188–205.

Comolli, Jean-Louis. "Chacun son soi." *Cahiers du cinéma* 197 (December 1967/January 1968): 51–54.

Coursodon, Jean-Pierre. "Jerry Lewis." In *American Directors.* Vol. 2. Ed. Jean-Pierre Coursodon and Pierre Sauvage. New York: McGraw-Hill, 1983. 189–200.

Daney, Serge. "*Which Way to the Front?*" *Cahiers du cinéma* 228 (March/April 1971): 60–61.

Deleuze, Gilles. *Cinéma 2: L'image temps.* Paris: Éditions de Minuit, 1985.

Deleuze, Gilles, and Félix Guattari. *Capitalisme et schizophrénie: Mille plateaux.* Paris: Éditions de Minuit, 1980.

Durgnat, Raymond. *The Crazy Mirror: Hollywood Comedy and the American Image*. New York: Horizon Press, 1970.

Garcia, Roger, ed. *Frank Tashlin*. Paris: Yellow Now, 1994.

Hamrah, A. S. "Aftermirth." *Bunnyhop* 8 (1997): 29–31.

———. "Thus Spake Cinderfella." In *The Factsheet Five Zine Reader*. Ed. R. Seth Friedman. New York: Three Rivers Press, 1997. 60–62.

Johnston, Claire, and Paul Willemen, eds. *Frank Tashlin*. Edinburgh: Edinburgh Film Festival, 1973.

Kite, B. "The Jerriad: A Clown Painting." Part 1. *The Believer* 7 (October 2003): 49–58; Part 2. *The Believer* 8 (November 2003): 52–60.

Kràl, Petr. *Le Burlesque, ou Morale de la tarte à la crème*. Paris: Éditions Ramsay, 2007.

Krutnik, Frank. *Inventing Jerry Lewis*. Washington, D.C.: Smithsonian Institution Press, 2000.

———. "Sex and Slapstick: The Martin and Lewis Phenomenon." In *Enfant Terrible! Jerry Lewis in American Film*. Ed. Murray Pomerance. New York: New York University Press, 2002. 109–21.

Leutrat, Jean-Louis, and Paul Simonci. *Jerry Lewis*. Premier Plan no. 36. Lyon: SERDOC, 1965.

Levy, Shawn. *King of Comedy: The Life and Art of Jerry Lewis*. New York: St. Martin's Press, 1996.

Lewis, Jerry. *The Total Film-Maker*. New York: Random House, 1971.

Lewis, Jerry, and Herb Gluck. *Jerry Lewis in Person*. New York: Atheneum, 1982.

Lewis, Jerry, and James Kaplan. *Dean and Me (A Love Story)*. New York: Doubleday, 2005.

Mago. "Souvenirs d'un film qui n'est jamais sorti." Rev. of *The Day the Clown Cried*. Trans. Catherine Masson. *Positif* 447 (May 1998): 65–68.

Marx, Karl. "Estranged Labor." In *Economic and Philosophic Manuscripts of 1844*. Trans. Martin Milligan. Ed. Dirk J. Struik. New York: International Publishers, 1964. 106–19.

Neibaur, James L., and Ted Okuda. *The Jerry Lewis Films: An Analytical Filmography of the Innovative Comic*. Jefferson, N.C.: McFarland and Co., 1995.

O'Brien, Geoffrey. *Dream Time: Chapters from the Sixties*. New York: Viking, 1988.

Oudart, Jean-Pierre. "Cinema and Suture." Trans. Kari Hanet. In *Cahiers du cinéma, 1969–1972: The Politics of Representation*. Ed. Nick Browne. Cambridge, Mass.: Harvard University Press, 1990. 45–57.

Partridge, Eric. *Origins: A Short Etymological Dictionary of Modern English*. New York: Greenwich House, 1983.

Polan, Dana. "Being and Nuttiness: Jerry Lewis and the French." *Journal of Popular Film* 12.1 (Spring 1984): 42–46.

———. "Working Hard Hardly Working: Labor and Leisure in the Films of

Jerry Lewis." In *Enfant Terrible! Jerry Lewis in American Film.* Ed. Murray Pomerance. New York: New York University Press, 2002. 211–23.

Pomerance, Murray, ed. *Enfant Terrible! Jerry Lewis in American Film.* New York: New York University Press, 2002.

————. "The Errant Boy." In *Enfant Terrible! Jerry Lewis in American Film.* Ed. Murray Pomerance. New York: New York University Press, 2002. 239–55.

Recasens, Gérard. *Jerry Lewis.* Cinéma d'aujourd'hui no. 59. Paris: Editions Seghers, 1970.

Rosenbaum, Jonathan. *Placing Movies: The Practice of Film Criticism.* Berkeley: University of California Press, 1995.

Sarris, Andrew. *The American Cinema: Directors and Directions 1929–1968.* New York: E. P. Dutton, 1968.

Simsolo, Noël. *Le monde de Jerry Lewis.* Paris: Editions du Cerf, 1969.

Tosches, Nick. *Dino: Living High in the Dirty Business of Dreams.* New York: Doubleday, 1992.

Index |

Adams, Stanley, 55
Adler, Jay, 67, 115
Adrian, Iris, 80, 112
ambiguity, 31, 44–46, 48, 76, 91
America, 75–76, 98
American in Paris, An (Minnelli film),
  119
Anderson, Judith, 105
Arizona Dream (Kusturica film), 9
Arnold, Edward, 113–14
Artists and Models (Tashlin film), 4
Atkins, Felicia, 55
authority, 62–64, 83, 84. *See also* disrup-
  tion; ideology
automotive culture, 76

Balin, Ina, 19, 43, 79, 107, 112
Ballard, Kaye, 68
Barnett, Vince, 77, 115
Basie, Count, 64, 96, 106
Bava, Mario, 12
Bay, Susan, 12
Bellboy, The, 4–5, 50, 76, 99, 117; black-
  and-white in, 5, 71, 72; characterizations and performances in, 19, 24, 28,
  37; and *Cracking Up,* 22, 23; duration
  and repetition in, 86, 87, 88, 90; fantasy
  and escape in, 44, 75, 76; formalism
  and materialism in, 14, 17, 87–88, 122;
  "Jerry Lewis" as character in, 26, 36,
  64, 79–80, 110; language in, 61, 64–65,
  66, 107; mise-en-scène of, 72, 73, 74–
  75, 79–80, 90; music in, 96; photogra-

phy in, 77; production of, 4–5, 114–15;
  prologue of, 5, 78; self-referentiality in,
  21, 22; silence in, 52, 62–63, 64, 93, 97;
  sound in, 94; subversion of orders in,
  58, 59–60; unconventionality of, 4–5,
  16; women in, 54–55, 89, 90; work in,
  28, 56–57, 61
Benayoun, Robert, 6, 53, 54, 91, 129
Ben Casey (TV series), 48
Benny, Jack, 116
Bergson, Henri, 93
Berle, Milton, 17, 22, 78
Best, James, 24, 36
Best Years of Our Lives, The (Wyler film),
  126
Big Mouth, The, 7, 15, 38, 66, 99; authority figures in, 62, 83; characterization
  of Clamson in, 20, 25–26, 27, 28, 49;
  comedians in, 21; communication in,
  12–13, 59, 63, 76; composition in, 81,
  83; and death, 29; delay and duration
  in, 87, 88–89; fantasy in, 75–76; as film
  of protest, 49–50; flight in, 14, 50–51;
  looks at the camera in, 41, 42; music in,
  96; order-words in, 58, 60; reactions to
  Lewis character in, 22, 40, 44; revenge
  in, 84; sentimentality in, 45, 49; voices
  in, 92, 97
black-and-white, 5, 71–72
Blanchot, Maurice, 15, 97, 98
blocks: characters as, 18, 20, 30, 63, 83;
  episodes as, 10, 15–18, 19, 75, 88; and
  order-words, 58–59; and set design,
  15–16. *See also* obstruction

"Blues in Hoss's Flat" (Count Basie record), 64, 73, 96
body, 17, 20, 37, 107; and composition, 83. *See also* identity
Boeing Boeing (Rich film), 6, 8, 54
Bold Ones, The (TV series), 48
Bolero (Ruggles film), 117
Bonjour Monsieur Lewis (Benayoun book), 6
"Boy," 9, 79
Broadway Rhythm (Del Ruth film), 119
Brooks, Mel, 121
Bukatman, Scott, 36, 96
Burlesque on Carmen (Chaplin film), 51
Butterworth, Donna, 6

Cabot, Sebastian, 18
Caddy, The (Taurog film), 19, 21
Cahiers du cinéma, 6
Callas, Charlie, 21, 40
camera movement, 103–4, 105, 106; in *The Bellboy,* 89; in "Boy," 79; in *The Errand Boy,* 73–74, 76, 78–79; in *The Ladies Man,* 16, 68, 73, 78, 84; in *The Nutty Professor,* 16, 40, 42, 68, 78; in *The Patsy,* 24, 83, 85; in *Three on a Couch,* 46, 81–82
Caprice (Tashlin film), 54
Captains Courageous (Fleming film), 118
Carmel, Roger C., 13
Carradine, John, 112
cartoon, 60, 105–6
Cassavetes, John, 9, 24, 40
Chaplin, Charles, 15, 19, 20, 33; pathos and seriousness in, 51, 107, 108, 109
childhood, 48, 49, 121
Cinderfella (Tashlin film), 4, 22, 52, 68, 119; ballroom scene, 31, 95–96, 106–7; Maximilian as unresponsive partner in, 34, 37, 38; Tashlin's direction of, 105–6
cinema: apparatus and technology of, 3, 30, 91–92, 103; as cultural institution and industry, 8–9, 59, 69, 71, 119; and dubbing, in *The Errand Boy,* 45–46, 92; video assist, 75. *See also* lens
Clayton, Bob, 24, 59
clown: in *The Day the Clown Cried,* 8, 14; in *The Errand Boy,* 44; in *The Fam-*

ily Jewels, 29, 51; in *Hardly Working,* 13, 14, 22, 29, 33; as mask, 110, 128
coherence, 15, 16, 34–35, 96, 120
Colgate Comedy Hour (TV show), 35–36
color, 70–72, 76, 118, 119
Columbia Pictures, 7
comedy: comic traditions, 1, 10, 64, 84, 97; gag construction, 17, 86–87, 91; and humor or lack of humor, 51, 76; and serious drama, 26–27, 48–49, 51–53, 108–11, 129; and therapy, 57
Comment vont les enfants? (omnibus film), 9
communication: failure of, 41–42, 59–60, 63, 76; and performance, 30; as theme, 12–13, 61–62. *See also* nonsense; speech; unresponsive partner
Comolli, Jean-Louis, 28
composition, 16, 42, 77–85, 117–18; and aspect ratio, 99n6; and time, 90
Conreid, Hans, 39
costume, 68, 70, 79, 89, 90
counterpoint, 124–25
Cracking Up, 9, 78, 88, 99, 133n1; authority figures in, 62; characterization in, 27, 28; and death, 29; ending of, 15, 23–24, 36, 55, 56; episodic structure of, 13–14, 77; flight in, 14, 34; music in, 96; order-words in, 58; parody of sentimentality in, 47–48; self-referentiality of, 22–23; space in, 23, 72, 75, 93; therapy in, 13; unconventionality of, 16; Warren as misfit in, 9, 13, 23, 42, 49
Crosby and Hope, 50
"Cure, The" (Chaplin film), 76
Curtis, Tony, 6, 54
cutting, 17, 68, 83, 86, 122. *See also* reverse shot

Daney, Serge, 16
Davis, Sammy, Jr., 8, 9, 47
Day the Clown Cried, The (unreleased film), 8, 14, 37
Dean and Me (Lewis and Kaplan book), 1, 51
death, 29, 48–49, 69, 72
delay, 37, 86–91

Deleuze, Gilles, 26, 28, 61, 99n5
Delicate Delinquent, The (McGuire film),
4, 5, 52, 96
desire, 68, 89–90
DeVol, Frank, 12
disaster, 14, 84–85. *See also* disruption
discontinuity, 18, 19, 28–29, 97–99; and
genre, 51; and reverse shot, 39. *See
also* disruption; fragmentation; gaps
Disorderly Orderly, The (Tashlin film), 6,
22, 41, 52; mummy gag in, 34; receptivity of Lewis character in, 28; revenge
and disaster in, 84, 85; Tashlin's direction of, 106, 107
disruption, 14, 34–35, 59, 67, 84–85; of
naturalism, 44; of plot, 10. *See also*
discontinuity
Donlevy, Brian, 31
Donner, Richard, 8
Don't Give Up the Ship (Taurog film),
4, 5
Don't Make Waves (Mackendrick film), 54
Don't Raise the Bridge, Lower the River
(Paris film), 7, 8
doubles. *See* duality
Douglas, Gordon, 7
Dream Time (O'Brien book), 54
Dr. Jekyll and Mr. Hyde (Mamoulian
film), 128–29
Dr. Jekyll and Mr. Hyde (Stevenson
novel), 6
*Dr. Strangelove or: How I Learned to
Stop Worrying and Love the Bomb*
(Kubrick film), 121
duality, 1–2, 34–36, 110. *See also* reverse
shot
dummies, 14, 34, 43, 57
duration, 12, 39, 86–91, 95, 111
Durgnat, Raymond, 88
Durocher, Leo, 47, 78

Edelman, Herb, 13
editing. *See* cutting
Edwards, Blake, 121
Edwards, Vincent, 48
episodic construction, 10–18, 19. *See also*
blocks
Errand Boy, The, 37, 76, 99, 108; black-
and-white in, 5, 71, 72; boardroom
scene, 28–29, 63–64, 66, 73–74, 96;
camera movement in, 73–74, 76,
78–79; chaos in, 84, 85; characterization of Morty in, 20, 28, 33, 46–47;
composition in, 78, 79, 80–81, 82, 85;
dubbing in, 45–46, 92, 123; ending of,
20, 26, 36, 56; filmmaking in, 3, 47, 59,
71, 119; language and speech in, 59,
60–61, 62, 65–66, 96–97; Magnolia in,
11, 44, 51, 55, 107; music in, 64, 68,
96; narrative of, 5, 11, 14, 16; orders
in, 58–59; performance in, 24, 30, 31;
recalled in later films, 22, 23; reverse
field in, 39, 43; self-referentiality in,
21, 98; sentimentality and seriousness
in, 46–47, 48, 49, 110; seriality in, 89;
silence in, 63–64; sound in, 92, 93, 94,
95; space in, 67, 73–74, 75, 78; suits of
armor in, 34, 43, 86; swimming-pool
scene, 73, 86, 90; women in, 55; work
in, 31–32, 57
escape, 14, 50, 55, 75, 82; cinema as,
69, 71
excess, 82, 85
exposition, 105, 108, 118, 125, 129

Faces (Cassavetes film), 9
family, 45, 46, 55–57
Family Jewels, The, 6, 16, 25, 36, 76;
camera lens in, 42, 43, 121; composition in, 83; and *Cracking Up,* 23; and
death, 29; delay in, 86; disruption
of plot in, 10; episodic structure of,
11–12, 18; home in, 56; language in,
58, 63, 97; multiplicity in, 28, 90, 98;
parade march in, 10, 11fig2, 15, 84;
photography in, 77; sentimentality in,
33, 47, 48; and *Singin' in the Rain,* 92;
sound in, 91, 92, 94; space in, 67, 72,
73, 75, 119; "This Diamond Ring" in,
46, 120; Uncle Everett in, 26, 29, 48,
51, 72
fantasy, 21, 31, 44, 50, 75–76; and cinema, 71; and music, 95–96; and space,
68; in *The Patsy,* 90–91
Feld, Fritz, 19
flight. *See* escape

fantasy, 96; in *The Patsy,* 76, 79, 96. *See also* singing
My Friend Irma (Marshall film), 3, 102

narrative. *See* plot
naturalism, 51, 68, 85, 98; and dialogue, 67; and *The Errand Boy,* 107; and fantasy, 44; and *The Ladies Man,* 46, 115; and lighting, 74; and music, 64; and psychology, 20, 87; and sound, 94. *See also* verisimilitude
Nicholson, Jack, 109–10
nonsense, 63, 93
North, Sheree, 103
Novelites, The, 21
Nutty Professor, The, 5–6, 50, 54, 84, 99; address to audience in, 44, 98, 107; attitudes toward Buddy Love in, 14, 48, 52, 131–33; camera movement in, 16, 40, 42, 68, 78; characterization in, 20, 131–33; color in, 70, 71, 72; composition in, 79, 82, 83; counterpoint in, 110, 124; delay in, 87; desire in, 89; home and family in, 55, 56; identity in, 26, 27, 33, 36, 131–32; insecurity in, 29, 49, 53; inspiration for and writing of, 128–30; language in, 61, 97; lighting in, 70, 74; looks and vision in, 40, 41, 42, 45, 121; masculinity in, 32; music in, 96; received as attack on Dean Martin, 130–31; receptivity of Kelp in, 28; sound in, 92, 94, 95; space in, 67, 68, 69–70; therapy in, 52, 57; transformation scene, 51; unresponsive partner in, 37

O'Brien, Geoffrey, 54
obstruction, 78–85
Oedipus complex, 55–56. *See also* family
Oliver, Susan, 33
Olivier, Laurence, 110
One More Time, 8, 9, 21, 45, 51; color in, 72; duration in, 88; friendship in, 36–37; multiplicity in, 90; reverse field in, 43; space in, 70, 78
order-words, 58–61, 99n5
Oudart, Jean-Pierre, 39

Pack Up Your Troubles (Marshall film), 102
Paramount Pictures, 2–7, 75, 105, 124
Paris, Jerry, 7
Parrish, Leslie, 27
Partridge, Eric, 15
pathos, 47, 51–52
Patsy, The, 3, 6, 52, 54, 99; camera movement in, 24, 83, 85; chaos and order in, 85; color in, 70, 72; composition in, 79, 83; Copa Café scene, 12, 39, 66, 90–91, 95; death in, 29; direction of actors in, 112; duration in, 12, 87, 90–91; *Ed Sullivan Show* scene, 21, 30–31, 43, 70, 85; ending of, 36, 43–44, 85; family in, 57; identity in, 19, 24, 26; language in, 37, 58, 61, 66; look at the camera in, 40, 41; music in, 76, 79, 96; narrative of, 14, 16; performance in, 30–31, 90, 127; pop culture in, 76; restaurant scene, 32–33; self-referentiality in, 21–22, 44, 98; sentimentality and seriousness in, 45, 49, 51, 107–8, 110; singing-lesson scene, 39, 87, 93–94, 111; sound, 92, 93–94, 95; space in, 67, 69, 70, 72, 74; unresponsive partner in, 37, 38; voice in, 97
Peckinpah, Sam, 121
performance, 18–33, 52, 74–75, 90, 126–28. *See also* actors
Pevney, Joseph, 51
phonograph, 92–93, 95
photography, 77
Pink Panther, The (Edwards film), 54
Pitnick, SanDee, 43, 126
plot, disruption or absence of, 4–5, 10–13, 16, 18, 91; as pretext, 11, 50
point of view, 42–43, 81. *See also* composition
Polan, Dana, 31
Pomerance, Murray, 97
Positif, 6
power, 62–64, 83, 84. *See also* disruption; ideology
psychoanalysis, 39, 55, 57. *See also* therapy
Public Enemy, The (Wellman film), 129
Pully, B. S., 66

That's My Boy (Walker film), 3, 19, 51, 52
"Their First Mistake" (Marshall film), 102
therapy: and cinema, 71; and comedy, 57; in *Cracking Up,* 13; and disaster, 84; in *The Ladies Man,* 10–11, 52; in *The Nutty Professor,* 52, 57; and pop psychology, 38, 65–66; in *Three on a Couch,* 12, 52–54. *See also* psychoanalysis
"This Diamond Ring" (Gary Lewis song), 46, 93, 120
Thousand Eyes of Dr. Mabuse, The (Lang film), 79
Three on a Couch, 12, 16, 29, 50, 58; James Best in, 24, 36; camera movement in, 46, 81–82; color in, 71, 72, 119; confession in, 44; dance scene in, 18, 46, 81–82; as departure for Lewis, 7, 26, 48, 49, 54; friendship in, 36; impersonations in, 18, 26–27, 28, 32, 97; language in, 20, 63, 124; mise-en-scène of, 81–82, 84–85; money in, 33; multiplicity in, 55, 89, 90; music in, 96; space in, 70, 72–73, 75; therapy in, 52–54; women in, 53, 55; writing of, 128
Three-Ring Circus (Pevney film), 51
Three Stooges, The, 111
time, 86–91. *See also* duration
Too Late Blues (Cassavetes film), 9
Total Film-Maker, The (Lewis book), 17, 78, 98
"Towed in a Hole" (Marshall film), 102
Tracy, Spencer, 118
transformation. *See* metamorphosis
Traubel, Helen, 24, 112
Twentieth Century–Fox, 7

United Artists, 8
United States, 75–76, 98
unresponsive partner, 34–35, 37, 88, 90. *See also* receptivity

Vacances de M. Hulot, Les (Tati film), 76
van Voorhis, Westbrook, 71, 77
verisimilitude, 16, 91. *See also* naturalism

Vidal, Gore, 4
video assist, 75
Visit to a Small Planet (Taurog film), 4, 5
voice. *See* speech

Wachsberger, Nat, 8
Walker, Hal, 3
Wallis, Hal, 4, 6
Walston, Ray, 84
Warhol, Andy, 76
Warner Bros., 8, 9
Way . . . Way Out (Douglas film), 7, 8
Weaver, Doodles, 86
What's New Pussycat? (Donner film), 54
Which Way to the Front? 8, 14, 21, 45, 48; as anti-sentimental, 46, 49; authority figure in, 62, 83; composition in, 81, 83; delay in, 87; flight in, 14; humor in, 51; independence from plot of, 16; Jewishness in, 64; language in, 56, 59, 61, 63, 64, 65; lighting in, 74; money in, 33, 49; music in, 96; Oedipal scenario of, 55, 56, 57; performance in, 18, 28, 31; phonograph in, 93; rejection theme in, 14, 31, 37, 58; self-insight in, 38; self-referentiality in, 22; space in, 68, 77; voice in, 97
Who's Minding the Store? (Tashlin film), 6, 21–22, 84, 85, 107
Wilder, Billy, 121
Winchell, Walter, 75
women, 10, 53, 54–55, 68, 89–90
Wood, John, 65
work, 18, 56–57, 61; and identity, 28, 31–33
World of Henry Orient, The (Hill film), 54
Wuthering Heights (Wyler film), 129
Wyler, William, 121, 126
Wynn, Ed, 119
Wynn, Keenan, 66, 112

You're Never Too Young (Taurog film), 35, 84

Zinnemann, Fred, 118, 121
zoom, 77, 78–79

Chris Fujiwara is the author of *The World and Its Double: The Life and Work of Otto Preminger* and *Jacques Tourneur: The Cinema of Nightfall*. He has edited several books, including *Defining Moments in Movies*. He has contributed articles on film to numerous anthologies and periodicals and is the editor of *Undercurrent* (www.fipresci.org/undercurrent), the online film-criticism magazine of the international film critics' association FIPRESCI. He has taught and lectured on film history and aesthetics at Tokyo University, the Athénée Français Cultural Center in Tokyo, Yale University, Rhode Island School of Design, Emerson College, and Temple University.

Books in the series Contemporary Film Directors

Nelson Pereira dos Santos
Darlene J. Sadlier

Abbas Kiarostami
Mehrnaz Saeed-Vafa and
Jonathan Rosenbaum

Joel and Ethan Coen
R. Barton Palmer

Claire Denis
Judith Mayne

Wong Kar-wai
Peter Brunette

Edward Yang
John Anderson

Pedro Almodóvar
Marvin D'Lugo

Chris Marker
Nora Alter

Abel Ferrara
Nicole Brenez, translated by
Adrian Martin

Jane Campion
Kathleen McHugh

Jim Jarmusch
Juan Suárez

Roman Polanski
James Morrison

Manoel de Oliveira
John Randal Johnson

Neil Jordan
Maria Pramaggiore

Paul Schrader
George Kouvaros

Jean-Pierre Jeunet
Elizabeth Ezra

Terrence Malick
Lloyd Michaels

Sally Potter
Catherine Fowler

Atom Egoyan
Emma Wilson

Albert Maysles
Joe McElhaney

Jerry Lewis
Chris Fujiwara

The University of Illinois Press
is a founding member of the
Association of American University Presses.

Composed in 10/13 New Caledonia
with Helvetica Neue display
by Celia Shapland
at the University of Illinois Press
Manufactured by Cushing-Malloy, Inc.

University of Illinois Press
1325 South Oak Street
Champaign, IL 61820-6903
www.press.uillinois.edu